W9-ASQ-533

Fix It Quick™

Favorite Brand Name™
SLOW COOKER

Publications International, Ltd.

Favorite Brand Name Recipes at www.fbnr.com

Copyright © 2004 Publications International, Ltd.
All rights reserved. This publication may not be reproduced or quoted in whole or in part by any means whatsoever without written permission from:

Louis Weber, CEO
Publications International, Ltd.
7373 North Cicero Avenue
Lincolnwood, IL 60712

Permission is never granted for commercial purposes.

Fix It Quick is a trademark of Publications International, Ltd.

Favorite Brand Name is a trademark of Publications International, Ltd

All recipes and photographs that contain specific brand names are copyrighted by those companies and/or associations, unless otherwise specified. All photographs copyright © Publications International, Ltd.

Some of the products listed in this publication may be in limited distribution.

Photography on pages 7, 10, 16, 17, 50, 75, 83, 107, 109, 111, 139, 171, 173, 177, 181 and 182 by Proffitt Photography, Ltd., Chicago.
Photographer: Laurie Proffitt
Photographer's Assistant: Gary Jochim
Food Stylist: Kim Hartman
Assistant Food Stylist: Alison Reich
Prop Stylist: Paula Walters

Pictured on the front cover: Simple Coq au Vin *(page 144).*
Pictured on the back cover *(left to right):* Slow-Cooked Korean Beef Short Ribs *(page 108),* Peach-Pecan Upside-Down Cake *(page 172)* and Spicy Asian Pork Filling *(page 138).*

ISBN: 0-7853-9681-0

Library of Congress Control Number: 2003109986

Manufactured in China.

8 7 6 5 4 3 2 1

Microwave Cooking: Microwave ovens vary in wattage. Use the cooking times as guidelines and check for doneness before adding more time.

Contents

Top to bottom: Vegetarian Sausage Rice (page 74), Mexicali Chicken (page 148) and Cherry Flan (page 170)

Take It Slow

It cooks dinner while you run errands, turns tough cuts of meat into succulent main courses and lets you have a pot roast on the table five minutes after you walk in the door. No, it's not a robot or a personal chef, it's your trusty slow cooker. Here are some tips to help you get the most out of a busy cook's best friend.

Peasant Potatoes (page 78)

Quick Tips and Simple Secrets

Manufacturers recommend filling your slow cooker between one-half to three-fourths full for best results.

Keep the lid on. The steam that develops in a tightly closed slow cooker is important to the cooking process (and to food safety). If you sneak a peak, the temperature is instantly lowered and takes about 20 minutes to recover.

Always taste dishes before serving them since spices and flavorings can be diluted with long slow cooking. Adjust seasonings or add fresh herbs shortly before serving.

Root vegetables like carrots and potatoes take longer to cook than meat. Cut them into small, uniform pieces and place them near the bottom or side of the slow cooker to solve the problem.

Add dairy products towards the end of the cooking time in order to avoid curdling.

Never place a hot crockery insert from a slow cooker on a cold surface. The sudden temperature change could cause cracking.

Slow cooking fades food's colors, so be ready to add interest with last-minute garnishes like chopped fresh herbs, citrus zest, diced tomatoes, red peppers, shredded cheese, or sour cream.

Meat Magic

Choose inexpensive, less tender cuts of meat for slow cooking (chuck, not filet mignon), since tender cuts fall apart and lose flavor.

Trim visible fat from meats, and, if possible, brown fatty cuts, such as ribs and ground meat, to cook off excess fat before adding to the slow cooker.

Brown poultry before slow cooking to add flavor and color to the finished dish. Remember that skin will not crisp in a slow cooker, so you may want to choose skinless cuts or remove the skin before serving.

Because slow cookers trap moisture, they can make sauces watery. To thicken sauces at the end of the cooking time, remove the solids from the cooker. Make a paste of ¼ cup each flour and water, or 2 tablespoons each cornstarch and water. Stir the paste into the cooking liquid, and cook on HIGH about 15 minutes until the mixture boils and thickens. Always taste the liquid before thickening, though. If it lacks flavor, you're better off simmering it uncovered on the stove to concentrate the flavor and thicken at the same time.

Safe and Slow

Slow cookers use low temperatures to cook foods safely, but this special cooking method requires some precautions.

If you prepare ingredients ahead of time, store meat and vegetables separately and keep them covered and refrigerated until you're ready to turn on the slow cooker.

Do not use your slow cooker to defrost and cook frozen foods. It could seriously change the recipe timing and increase the amount of time needed to heat ingredients to a safe temperature.

Veal Stew with Horseradish (page 130)

Don't leave a finished dish in the slow cooker for a long time with the heat off. If you're not at home and a power outage occurs while the slow cooker is on, discard the food even if it looks done. If you are at home, finish cooking the ingredients on the stove or by some other means.

It's best not to reheat leftovers in a slow cooker since they might take too long to reach a safe temperature. Instead, heat the food on a stove until it is steaming and then transfer it to a preheated slow cooker for serving.

Dips and Other Delights

Invite a slow cooker to your next party. Whether you're serving a dip, chicken wings or mulled wine, a slow cooker not only makes preparation a snap, it keeps munchies hot and handy on the buffet table.

Chunky Pinto Bean Dip

2 cans (15 ounces each) pinto beans, rinsed and drained
1 can (14½ ounces) Mexican-style diced tomatoes, drained
1 cup chopped onion
⅔ cup chunky salsa
1 tablespoon vegetable oil
1½ teaspoons minced garlic
1 teaspoon ground coriander
1 teaspoon ground cumin
1½ cups (6 ounces) shredded Mexican cheese blend or shredded Cheddar cheese
¼ cup chopped cilantro
Blue corn or other tortilla chips
Assorted raw vegetables
Sour cream and cilantro for garnish

1. Combine beans, tomatoes, onion, salsa, oil, garlic, coriander and cumin in slow cooker. Cover; cook on LOW 5 to 6 hours or until onion is tender.

2. Partially mash bean mixture with potato masher. Stir in cheese and cilantro. Garnish and serve at room temperature with chips and vegetables.   *Makes about 5 cups*

Chunky Pinto Bean Dip

Maple-Glazed Meatballs

1½ cups ketchup
1 cup maple syrup or maple-flavored syrup
⅓ cup reduced-sodium soy sauce
1 tablespoon quick-cooking tapioca
1½ teaspoons ground allspice
1 teaspoon dry mustard
2 packages (about 16 ounces each) frozen fully-cooked meatballs
1 can (20 ounces) pineapple chunks, drained

1. Stir together ketchup, syrup, soy sauce, tapioca, allspice and mustard in slow cooker.

2. Partially thaw and separate meatballs. Carefully stir meatballs and pineapple chunks into ketchup mixture. Cover; cook on LOW 5 to 6 hours. Stir before serving. Serve with cocktail picks. *Makes about 48 meatballs*

Variation: Serve over hot cooked rice for an entrée.

Creamy Cheesy Spinach Dip

2 packages (10 ounces each) frozen chopped spinach, thawed
2 cups chopped onions
1 teaspoon salt
½ teaspoon garlic powder
¼ teaspoon black pepper
12 ounces processed cheese with jalapeño peppers, cubed
Assorted crackers (optional)
Cherry tomatoes with pulp removed (optional)

1. Drain spinach and squeeze dry, reserving ¾ cup liquid. Place spinach, reserved liquid, onions, salt, garlic powder and pepper into slow cooker; stir to blend. Cover; cook on HIGH 1½ hours.

2. Stir in cheese and cook 30 minutes longer or until melted. Serve with crackers or use to fill cherry tomato shells. *Makes about 4 cups*

Easy Does It

To thaw spinach quickly, remove outer paper wrapper and place cardboard containers in microwave without unwrapping further. Microwave at HIGH (100%) 3 to 4 minutes or until just thawed.

Maple-Glazed Meatballs

Spicy Sweet & Sour Cocktail Franks

  2 packages (8 ounces each) cocktail franks
½ cup ketchup or chili sauce
½ cup apricot preserves
  1 teaspoon hot pepper sauce
   Additional hot pepper sauce, if desired

1. Combine all ingredients in slow cooker; mix well. Cover; cook on LOW 2 to 3 hours.

2. Serve warm or at room temperature with cocktail picks and additional hot pepper sauce, if desired.   *Makes about 4 dozen cocktail franks*

Spicy Sweet & Sour Cocktail Franks

Festive Bacon & Cheese Dip

  2 packages (8 ounces each) cream cheese, softened and cut into cubes
  4 cups (16 ounces) shredded Colby-Jack cheese
  1 cup half & half
  2 tablespoons prepared mustard
  1 tablespoon chopped onion
  2 teaspoons Worcestershire sauce
½ teaspoon salt
¼ teaspoon hot pepper sauce
  1 pound bacon, cooked and crumbled

Place cream cheese, Colby-Jack cheese, half & half, mustard, onion, Worcestershire sauce, salt and hot pepper sauce in slow cooker. Cover and cook, stirring occasionally, on LOW 1 hour or until cheese melts. Stir in bacon; adjust seasonings, if desired. Serve with crusty bread or fruit and vegetable dippers.

Makes about 1 quart

Hot Mulled Cider

½ gallon apple cider
½ cup packed light brown sugar
1½ teaspoons balsamic or cider vinegar
  1 teaspoon vanilla
  1 cinnamon stick
  6 whole cloves
½ cup applejack or bourbon (optional)

Combine all ingredients in slow cooker. Cover; cook on LOW 5 to 6 hours. Remove and discard cinnamon stick and cloves. Serve hot in mugs.

Makes 16 servings

Festive Bacon & Cheese Dip

Party Mix

3 cups bite-size rice cereal
2 cups O-shaped oat cereal
2 cups bite-size shredded wheat cereal
1 cup peanuts or pistachios
1 cup thin pretzel sticks
½ cup (1 stick) butter, melted
1 tablespoon Worcestershire sauce
1 teaspoon seasoned salt
½ teaspoon garlic powder
⅛ teaspoon ground red pepper (optional)

1. Combine cereals, nuts and pretzels in slow cooker.

2. Mix melted butter, Worcestershire sauce, seasoned salt, garlic powder and red pepper in small bowl. Pour over cereal mixture in slow cooker; toss lightly to coat.

Party Mix

3. Cover; cook on LOW 3 hours, stirring well every 30 minutes. Remove cover; cook 30 minutes more. Store in airtight container.

Makes 10 cups

Honey-Mustard Chicken Wings

3 pounds chicken wings
1 teaspoon salt
1 teaspoon black pepper
½ cup honey
½ cup barbecue sauce
2 tablespoons spicy brown mustard
1 clove garlic, minced
3 to 4 thin lemon slices

1. Rinse chicken and pat dry. Cut off wing tips; discard. Cut each wing at joint to make two pieces. Sprinkle salt and pepper on both sides of chicken. Place wing pieces on broiler rack. Broil 4 to 5 inches from heat about 10 minutes, turning halfway through cooking. Place broiled chicken wings in slow cooker.

2. Combine honey, barbecue sauce, mustard and garlic in small bowl; mix well. Pour sauce over chicken wings. Top with lemon slices. Cover; cook on LOW 4 to 5 hours.

3. Remove and discard lemon slices. Serve wings with sauce.   *Makes about 24 appetizers*

Honey-Mustard Chicken Wings

Creamy Artichoke-Parmesan Dip

2 cans (14 ounces each) artichoke hearts, drained and chopped
2 cups (8 ounces) shredded mozzarella cheese
1½ cups grated Parmesan cheese
1½ cups mayonnaise
½ cup finely chopped onion
½ teaspoon dried oregano leaves
¼ teaspoon garlic powder
Pita wedges
Assorted cut-up vegetables

1. Place all ingredients except pita wedges and vegetables into slow cooker; stir to blend well. Cover; cook on LOW 2 hours.

2. Serve with pita wedges and vegetables.

Makes 4 cups dip

Reuben Dip

1 jar or bag (about 32 ounces) sauerkraut, drained
2 cups shredded Swiss cheese
3 packages (2½ ounces each) corned beef, shredded
½ cup (1 stick) margarine, melted
1 egg, beaten
Rye cocktail bread or crackers

1. Combine all ingredients except rye bread in slow cooker. Cover; cook on HIGH 2 hours.

2. Serve with rye cocktail bread.

Makes 12 servings

Warm & Spicy Fruit Punch

4 cinnamon sticks
1 orange
1 teaspoon whole allspice
½ teaspoon whole cloves
7 cups water
1 can (12 ounces) frozen cranberry-raspberry juice concentrate, thawed
1 can (6 ounces) frozen lemonade concentrate, thawed
2 cans (5½ ounces each) apricot nectar

1. Break cinnamon into pieces. Using vegetable peeler, remove strips of orange peel. Squeeze juice from orange. Set aside.

2. Tie cinnamon, orange peel, allspice and cloves in cheesecloth bag.

3. Combine reserved orange juice, water, concentrates and apricot nectar in slow cooker; add spice bag. Cover; cook on LOW 5 to 6 hours.

4. Remove and discard spice bag.

Makes about 14 (6-ounce) servings

Easy Does It

Tying whole spices and other flavorings together in a cheesecloth bag makes them easy to remove before serving.

Creamy Artichoke-Parmesan Dip

Slow Cooker Cheese Dip

1 pound ground beef
1 pound Italian sausage
1 package (1 pound) processed cheese,
   cubed
1 can (11 ounces) sliced jalapeño peppers,
   drained
1 medium onion, diced
½ pound Cheddar cheese, cubed
1 package (8 ounces) cream cheese, cubed
1 container (8 ounces) cottage cheese
1 container (8 ounces) sour cream
1 can (8 ounces) diced tomatoes, drained
3 cloves garlic, minced
   Salt and pepper

1. Stir and cook ground beef and sausage in a medium skillet over medium-high heat; drain. Transfer to slow cooker.

2. Add processed cheese, jalapeño peppers, onion, Cheddar cheese, cream cheese, cottage cheese, sour cream, tomatoes and garlic to slow cooker. Season with salt and pepper.

3. Cover; cook on HIGH 1½ to 2 hours or until cheeses are melted. Serve with crackers or tortilla chips.   *Makes 16 to 18 servings*

Chai Tea

2 quarts (8 cups) water
8 bags black tea
¾ cup granulated sugar*
16 whole cloves
16 whole cardamom seeds, pods removed
   (optional)
5 cinnamon sticks
8 slices fresh ginger
1 cup milk

Chai Tea is typically a sweet drink. For less sweet tea, reduce sugar to ½ cup.

1. Combine all ingredients except milk in slow cooker. Cover; cook on HIGH 2 to 2½ hours.

2. Strain mixture; discard solids. (At this point, tea may be covered and refrigerated up to 3 days).

3. Stir in milk just before serving. Serve warm or chilled.   *Makes 8 to 10 servings*

Slow Cooker Cheese Dip

Chai Tea

Mulled Apple Cider

2 quarts bottled apple cider or juice (not unfiltered)
¼ cup packed light brown sugar
1 square (8 inches) double-thickness cheesecloth
8 allspice berries
4 cinnamon sticks, broken into halves
12 whole cloves
1 large orange
Additional cinnamon sticks (optional)

1. Combine apple cider and brown sugar in slow cooker. Rinse cheesecloth; squeeze out water. Wrap allspice berries and cinnamon stick halves in cheesecloth; tie securely with cotton string or strip of cheesecloth. Stick cloves randomly into orange; cut orange into quarters. Place spice bag and orange quarters in cider mixture.

2. Cover and cook on HIGH 2½ to 3 hours. Once cooked, cider may be turned to LOW and kept warm up to 3 additional hours. Remove and discard spice bag and orange before serving; ladle cider into mugs. Garnish with additional cinnamon sticks, if desired. *Makes 10 servings*

Tip: To make inserting cloves into the orange a little easier, first pierce the orange skin with the point of wooden skewer. Remove the skewer and insert a clove.

Brats in Beer

1½ pounds bratwurst links (about 5 or 6)
1 can or bottle (12 ounces) beer (not dark)
1 medium onion, thinly sliced
2 tablespoons brown sugar
2 tablespoons red wine or cider vinegar
Mustard
Cocktail rye bread

1. Place bratwurst, beer, onion, sugar and vinegar in slow cooker. Cover; cook on LOW 4 to 5 hours.

2. Remove bratwurst from cooking liquid. Cut into ½-inch-thick slices. For mini open-faced sandwiches, spread mustard on cocktail rye bread. Top with bratwurst slices.
Makes 10 to 15 appetizer servings

Easy Does It

A slow cooker makes a good extra burner when entertaining. Plug it in near the serving area to keep drinks or hors d'oeuvres hot and available for guests. The stove will be free to finish the rest of the cooking.

Brats in Beer

Honey-Sauced Chicken Wings

3 pounds chicken wings
1 teaspoon salt
½ teaspoon black pepper
1 cup honey
½ cup soy sauce
¼ cup chopped onions
¼ cup ketchup
2 tablespoons vegetable oil
2 cloves garlic, minced
¼ teaspoon red pepper flakes
   Toasted sesame seeds (optional)

1. Rinse chicken and pat dry. Cut off and discard wing tips. Cut each wing at joint to make two sections. Sprinkle wing parts with salt and pepper. Place wings on broiler pan. Broil 4 to 5 inches from heat 20 minutes, 10 minutes a side or until chicken is brown. Place chicken into slow cooker.

2. For sauce, combine honey, soy sauce, onions, ketchup, oil, garlic and pepper flakes in bowl. Pour over chicken wings. Cover; cook on LOW 4 to 5 hours or on HIGH 2 to 2½ hours. Garnish with sesame seeds, if desired.

Makes about 32 appetizers

Easy Taco Dip

½ pound ground beef chuck
1 cup frozen corn
½ cup chopped onion
½ cup salsa
½ cup mild taco sauce
1 can (4 ounces) diced mild green chilies
1 can (4 ounces) sliced ripe olives, drained
1 cup (4 ounces) shredded Mexican blend cheese
Tortilla chips
Sour cream

1. Cook meat in large nonstick skillet over medium-high heat until no longer pink, stirring to separate; drain. Spoon into slow cooker.

2. Add corn, onion, salsa, taco sauce, chilies and olives to slow cooker; stir to combine. Cover; cook on LOW 2 to 4 hours.

3. Just before serving, stir in cheese. Serve with tortilla chips and sour cream.

Makes about 3 cups dip

Tip: To keep this delicious dip hot through your entire party, simply leave it in the slow cooker on LOW.

Honey-Sauced Chicken Wings

Easy Taco Dip

Barbecued Meatballs

2 pounds lean ground beef
1⅓ cups ketchup, divided
3 tablespoons seasoned dry bread crumbs
1 egg, lightly beaten
2 tablespoons dried onion flakes
¾ teaspoon garlic salt
½ teaspoon black pepper
1 cup packed light brown sugar
1 can (6 ounces) tomato paste
¼ cup reduced-sodium soy sauce
¼ cup cider vinegar
1½ teaspoons hot pepper sauce
Diced bell peppers (optional)

1. Preheat oven to 350°F. Combine ground beef, ⅓ cup ketchup, bread crumbs, egg, onion flakes, garlic salt and black pepper in medium bowl. Mix lightly but thoroughly; shape into 1-inch meatballs. Place meatballs in two 15×10-inch jelly-roll pans or shallow roasting pans. Bake 18 minutes or until browned. Transfer meatballs to slow cooker.

2. Mix remaining 1 cup ketchup, sugar, tomato paste, soy sauce, vinegar and hot pepper sauce in medium bowl. Pour over meatballs. Cover; cook on LOW 4 hours. Serve with cocktail picks. Garnish with diced bell peppers, if desired.

Makes about 4 dozen meatballs

Parmesan Ranch Snack Mix

3 cups bite-size corn or rice cereal
2 cups oyster crackers
1 package (5 ounces) bagel chips, broken in half
1½ cups pretzel twists
1 cup pistachios
2 tablespoons grated Parmesan cheese
¼ cup butter, melted
1 package (1 ounce) dry ranch salad dressing mix
½ teaspoon garlic powder

1. Combine cereal, oyster crackers, bagel chips, pretzels, pistachios and Parmesan cheese in slow cooker; mix gently.

2. Combine butter, salad dressing mix and garlic powder in small bowl. Pour over cereal mixture; toss lightly to coat. Cover; cook on LOW 3 hours. Remove cover and stir gently. Continue to cook, uncovered, on LOW 30 minutes.

Makes about 9½ cups

Easy Does It

Invent a signature snack mix in your slow cooker. Start with the recipe above and substitute some of your family's favorite seasonings and goodies for the ones suggested.

Parmesan Ranch Snack Mix

Easiest Three-Cheese Fondue

**2 cups (8 ounces) shredded mild or sharp
    Cheddar cheese**
¾ cup reduced-fat (2%) milk
½ cup (2 ounces) crumbled blue cheese
**1 package (3 ounces) cream cheese, cut
    into cubes**
¼ cup finely chopped onion
1 tablespoon all-purpose flour
1 tablespoon margarine
2 cloves garlic, minced
4 to 6 drops hot pepper sauce
⅛ teaspoon ground red pepper
    **Breadsticks and assorted fresh
    vegetables for dipping**

1. Combine all ingredients except breadsticks and vegetables in slow cooker. Cover; cook on LOW 2 to 2½ hours, stirring once or twice, until cheese is melted and smooth.

2. Increase heat to HIGH and cook 1 to 1½ hours or until heated through. Serve with breadsticks and fresh vegetables. Garnish as desired.   *Makes 8 servings*

Lighten Up: To reduce the total fat, replace the Cheddar cheese and cream cheese with reduced-fat Cheddar and cream cheeses.

Mulled Cranberry Tea

2 tea bags
1 cup boiling water
1 bottle (48 ounces) cranberry juice
½ cup dried cranberries (optional)
⅓ cup sugar
1 large lemon, cut into ¼-inch slices
4 cinnamon sticks
6 whole cloves
    Additional thin lemon slices, for garnish
    Additional cinnamon sticks, for garnish

1. Place tea bags in slow cooker. Pour boiling water over tea bags; cover and let stand 5 minutes. Remove and discard tea bags. Stir in cranberry juice, cranberries, if desired, sugar, lemon slices, 4 cinnamon sticks and cloves. Cover; cook on HIGH 1 to 2 hours or on LOW 2 to 3 hours.

2. Remove and discard lemon slices, cinnamon sticks and cloves. Serve in warm mugs with additional fresh lemon slice and cinnamon stick.
    Makes 8 servings

Mulled Cranberry Tea

Campbell's® Nacho Chicken & Rice Wraps

**2 cans (10¾ ounces each) CAMPBELL'S®
    Condensed Cheddar Cheese Soup
1 cup water
2 cups PACE® Chunky Salsa *or* Picante
    Sauce
1¼ cups *uncooked* regular long-grain white
    rice
2 pounds skinless, boneless chicken
    breasts, cut into cubes
10 flour tortillas (10-inch)**

1. In slow cooker mix soup, water, salsa, rice and chicken. Cover and cook on **low** 7 to 8 hours or until chicken and rice are done.

2. Spoon **about 1 cup** rice mixture down center of each tortilla.

3. Fold opposite sides of tortilla over filling. Roll up from bottom. Cut each wrap in half.
Makes 10 servings

Variation: For firmer rice, substitute converted rice for regular.

Spiced Apple Tea

**3 bags cinnamon herbal tea
3 cups boiling water
2 cups unsweetened apple juice
6 whole cloves
1 cinnamon stick**

Place tea bags in slow cooker. Pour boiling water over tea bags; cover and let stand 10 minutes. Remove and discard tea bags. Add apple juice, cloves and cinnamon stick to slow cooker. Cover; cook on LOW 2 to 3 hours. Remove and discard cloves and cinnamon stick. Serve warm in mugs.
Makes 4 servings

Sausage Dip

**1 pound bulk sausage, cooked
1 pound processed American cheese
1 pound Mexican-flavored processed
    cheese
1 can (16 ounces) refried beans
1 can (10¾ ounces) condensed cream of
    mushroom soup
1 small onion, chopped
    Tortilla chips**

Place all ingredients except tortilla chips in slow cooker. Cover; cook on LOW about 2 hours or until heated through. Serve with tortilla chips.
Makes 20 servings

Bottom to top: Campbell's® Nacho Chicken & Rice Wraps,
Campbell's® Creamy Chicken & Wild Rice (page 158)

Mulled Wine

2 bottles (750 mL each) dry red wine, such
　　as Cabernet Sauvignon
1 cup light corn syrup
1 cup water
1 square (8 inches) double-thickness
　　cheesecloth
　Peel of 1 large orange
1 cinnamon stick, broken into halves
8 whole cloves
1 whole nutmeg

Combine wine, corn syrup and water in slow cooker. Rinse cheesecloth; squeeze out water. Wrap orange peel, cinnamon stick halves, cloves and nutmeg in cheesecloth. Tie bag securely with cotton string or strip of cheesecloth. Add to slow cooker. Cover; cook on HIGH 2 to 2½ hours. Remove and discard spice bag; ladle wine into mugs. Garnish as desired.

Makes 12 servings

Pizza Fondue

½ pound bulk Italian sausage
1 cup chopped onion
2 jars (26 ounces each) meatless pasta
　　sauce
4 ounces thinly sliced ham, finely chopped
1 package (3 ounces) sliced pepperoni,
　　finely chopped
¼ teaspoon red pepper flakes
1 pound mozzarella cheese, cut into
　　¾-inch cubes
1 loaf Italian or French bread, cut into
　　1-inch cubes

1. Cook sausage and onion in large skillet until sausage is browned. Drain off fat.

2. Transfer sausage mixture to slow cooker. Stir in pasta sauce, ham, pepperoni and pepper flakes. Cover; cook on LOW 3 to 4 hours.

3. Serve sauce with cheese cubes, bread cubes and fondue forks.

Makes 20 to 25 appetizer servings

Mulled Wine

Pizza Fondue

Meatballs in Burgundy Sauce

60 frozen prepared fully-cooked meatballs
3 cups chopped onions
1½ cups water
1 cup red wine
2 packages (about 1 ounce each) beef gravy mix
¼ cup ketchup
1 tablespoon dried oregano leaves
Hot cooked noodles

1. Combine all ingredients except noodles in slow cooker; stir to blend. Cover; cook on HIGH 5 hours.

2. Serve with noodles. *Makes 6 to 8 servings*

Meatballs in Burgundy Sauce

Mocha Supreme

2 quarts strong brewed coffee
½ cup instant hot chocolate beverage mix
1 cinnamon stick, broken into halves
1 cup whipping cream
1 tablespoon powdered sugar

1. Place coffee, hot chocolate mix and cinnamon stick halves in slow cooker; stir. Cover; cook on HIGH 2 to 2½ hours or until hot. Remove and discard cinnamon stick halves.

2. Beat cream in medium bowl with electric mixer on high speed until soft peaks form. Add powdered sugar; beat until stiff peaks form. Ladle hot beverage into mugs; top with whipped cream. *Makes 8 servings*

Note: To whip cream quickly, chill the bowl and beaters for about 15 minutes in the freezer and make sure the cream is cold, too. If there's no time for the freezer, chill the bowl with the cream by placing it into a bigger bowl filled with ice water. To reduce spatters, start the mixer at low or medium and gradually increase the speed.

Mocha Supreme

Hot & Hearty Bowls

Chili, chowder, soup and stew are naturals for slow cooking. Flavors have time to blend and you have time to take care of other things. Assemble ingredients in the morning and come home to the welcoming aroma of a hearty dinner.

Red Bean Soup with Andouille Sausage

2 tablespoons unsalted butter
1 large sweet onion, diced
2 large cloves garlic, chopped
3 stalks celery, diced
1 ham hock
1½ cups dried red kidney beans, soaked in cold water 1 hour, drained and rinsed
1 bay leaf
8 cups chicken stock
1 pound andouille smoked sausage, or other pork sausage, cut into ½-inch pieces
1 sweet potato, diced
2 parsnips, diced
  Salt and pepper to taste

1. Melt butter in large saucepan over medium heat. Add onion, garlic and celery. Cook and stir 5 minutes. Add to slow cooker along with ham hock, kidney beans, bay leaf; pour in chicken stock. Cover; cook on HIGH 2 hours.

2. Remove ham hock and discard. Cover; cook 2 hours more. Add sausage, sweet potato and parsnips. Cover; cook 30 minutes more or until kidney beans are soft. Season with salt and pepper.   *Makes 6 to 8 servings*

Note: Use a 6-quart slow cooker for this recipe. If using a smaller cooker, cut recipe ingredients in half.

Red Bean Soup with Andouille Sausage

Greek-Style Chicken Stew

2 cups sliced mushrooms
2 cups peeled cubed eggplant
1¼ cups reduced-sodium chicken broth
¾ cup coarsely chopped onion
2 cloves garlic, minced
1½ teaspoons all-purpose flour
1 teaspoon dried oregano leaves
½ teaspoon dried basil leaves
½ teaspoon dried thyme leaves
6 skinless chicken breasts, about 2 pounds
  Additional all-purpose flour
3 tablespoons dry sherry or reduced-
  sodium chicken broth
¼ teaspoon salt
¼ teaspoon black pepper
1 can (14 ounces) artichoke hearts, drained
12 ounces uncooked wide egg noodles

1. Combine mushrooms, eggplant, broth, onion, garlic, flour, oregano, basil and thyme in slow cooker. Cover; cook on HIGH 1 hour.

2. Coat chicken very lightly with flour. Generously spray large nonstick skillet with cooking spray; heat over medium heat until hot. Cook chicken 10 to 15 minutes or until browned on all sides.

3. Remove vegetables to bowl with slotted spoon. Layer chicken in slow cooker; return vegetables to slow cooker. Add sherry, salt and pepper. Reduce heat to LOW. Cover; cook 6 to 6½ hours or until chicken is no longer pink in center and vegetables are tender.

4. Stir in artichokes; cover and cook 45 minutes to 1 hour or until heated through. Cook noodles according to package directions. Serve chicken stew over noodles. *Makes 6 servings*

Mushroom Barley Stew

1 tablespoon olive oil
1 medium onion, finely chopped
1 cup chopped carrots (about 2 carrots)
1 clove garlic, minced
1 cup pearl barley
1 cup dried wild mushrooms, broken into
  pieces
1 teaspoon salt
½ teaspoon black pepper
½ teaspoon dried thyme leaves
5 cups vegetable broth

1. Heat oil in medium skillet over medium-high heat. Add onion, carrots and garlic; cook and stir 5 minutes or until tender. Place in slow cooker.

2. Add barley, mushrooms, salt, pepper and thyme. Stir in broth. Cover; cook on LOW 6 to 7 hours. Adjust seasonings, if desired.
Makes 4 to 6 servings

Easy Does It

To turn this thick robust stew into a soup, add 2 to 3 additional cups of broth. Cook the same length of time.

Mushroom Barley Stew

Potato & Spinach Soup with Gouda

Soup

   9 medium Yukon Gold potatoes, peeled
      and chopped into small cubes (about
      6 cups)
   2 cans (14 ounces) chicken broth
   ½ cup water
   1 small red onion, finely diced
   5 ounces baby spinach leaves
   ½ teaspoon salt
   ¼ teaspoon ground red pepper
   ¼ teaspoon black pepper
 2½ cups shredded smoked Gouda cheese,
      divided
   1 can (12 ounces) evaporated milk

Garnish

   4 tablespoons olive oil
   4 cloves garlic, cut into thin slices
   5 to 7 sprigs parsley, chopped

1. Combine potatoes, chicken broth, water, red onion, spinach, salt, red pepper and black pepper in slow cooker. Cover; cook on LOW 10 hours or until potatoes are tender.

2. Slightly mash potatoes in slow cooker; add 2 cups smoked Gouda and evaporated milk. Cover; cook on HIGH 15 to 20 minutes or until cheese is melted.

3. Cook and stir olive oil and garlic in small saucepan over low heat until golden brown; set aside. Pour soup into bowls. Sprinkle 2 to 3 teaspoons remaining Gouda cheese in each bowl. Add spoonful of garlic in center of each bowl; sprinkle with parsley.

Makes 8 to 10 servings

Lamb Meatball & Bean Soup

   1 pound ground lamb
   ¼ cup chopped onion
   1 clove garlic, minced
   1 teaspoon ground cumin
   ½ teaspoon salt
   2 cups chicken broth
   1 package (10 ounces) frozen chopped
      broccoli*
   1 can (14½ ounces) diced tomatoes,
      drained
   1 can (15 ounces) chick peas or black-eyed
      peas, drained
   ½ teaspoon dried thyme leaves, crushed
      Salt and black pepper

*1½ cups fresh broccoli florets may be substituted for 10-ounce package frozen chopped broccoli.

Combine lamb, onion, garlic, cumin and salt; mix lightly. Shape into 1-inch balls.** Brown meatballs in large skillet over medium-high heat, turning occasionally.

Place broth, broccoli, tomatoes, beans, thyme and meatballs in slow cooker. Cook on LOW 4 to 5 hours. Season to taste with salt and black pepper.

Makes 4 to 6 servings

**To quickly shape uniform meatballs, place meat mixture on cutting board; pat evenly into large square, 1 inch thick. With sharp knife, cut meat into 1-inch squares; shape each square into a ball.

Potato & Spinach Soup with Gouda

Double-Hearty, Double-Quick Veggie Chili

2 cans (15½ ounces each) dark kidney beans, rinsed and drained
1 package (16 ounces) frozen bell pepper stir-fry mixture or 2 bell peppers, chopped
1 cup frozen corn kernels
1 can (14½ ounces) diced tomatoes with peppers, celery and onions
3 tablespoons chili powder or to taste
2 teaspoons ground cumin, divided
2 teaspoons sugar
½ teaspoon salt
1 tablespoon extra virgin olive oil
Sour cream
Chopped cilantro leaves

1. In colander, combine beans, frozen pepper mixture and corn. Run under cold water until beans are well rinsed. Shake off excess water and place in slow cooker. If using fresh bell peppers, add 1 small onion, chopped.

2. Add tomatoes, chili powder, 1½ teaspoons cumin and sugar. Cover; cook on HIGH 3 hours or on LOW 5 hours.

3. Stir in salt, remaining ½ teaspoon cumin and olive oil. Serve with sour cream and cilantro.

Makes 4 to 6 servings

Summer Squash Stew

4 cans (14½ ounces each) diced seasoned tomatoes
2 pounds cooked Italian turkey sausage or diced cooked chicken
5 medium yellow squash, thinly sliced
5 medium zucchini, thinly sliced
1 red onion, finely chopped
2 tablespoons dried Italian herb mixture
1 tablespoon dried tomato, basil and garlic salt-free spice mixture
4 cups (16 ounces) shredded Mexican cheese blend

1. Combine all ingredients except cheese in slow cooker. Cover; cook on LOW 3 hours.

2. Top stew with cheese and cook an additional 15 minutes or until cheese melts.

Makes 6 servings

Double-Hearty, Double-Quick Veggie Chili

Summer Squash Stew

Mediterranean Lentil Soup

2 tablespoons olive oil
1 large sweet onion, diced
1 stalk celery, chopped
2 large cloves garlic, finely minced
1 tablespoon tomato paste
1 can (28 ounces) peeled whole plum
    tomatoes, drained and chopped
1½ teaspoons dried thyme
1½ cups dried lentils, soaked* in cold water
    1 hour, drained and rinsed
6 cups beef broth
2 bay leaves

Vinaigrette
2 tablespoons red wine vinegar
⅓ cup olive oil
2 tablespoons minced fresh parsley leaves
¾ cup packed fresh basil leaves
    Salt and black pepper

*Add 1 to 2 hours to cooking time if you do not soak lentils before cooking.

1. Heat olive oil in large saucepan over medium heat. Add onion, celery and garlic. Cook and stir 5 minutes until softened but not browned.

2. Stir in tomato paste, tomatoes, thyme and lentils. Add lentil mixture to slow cooker along with beef broth and bay leaves. Cover; cook on HIGH 4 hours or on LOW 8 hours or until lentils are soft.

3. To prepare vinaigrette, combine vinegar, oil, parsley and basil in blender or food processor. Process on high speed until smooth; set aside.

4. Season with salt and pepper. Stir vinaigrette into soup just before serving.

Makes 4 to 6 servings

White Bean Chili

Nonstick cooking spray
1 pound ground chicken
3 cups coarsely chopped celery
1 can (16 ounces) whole tomatoes,
    undrained and coarsely chopped
1 can (15½ ounces) Great Northern beans,
    drained and rinsed
1½ cups coarsely chopped onions
1 cup chicken broth
3 cloves garlic, minced
4 teaspoons chili powder
1½ teaspoons ground cumin
¾ teaspoon ground allspice
¾ teaspoon ground cinnamon
½ teaspoon black pepper

1. Spray large nonstick skillet with nonstick cooking spray; heat over high heat until hot. Add chicken; cook until browned, breaking into pieces with fork.

2. Combine chicken, celery, tomatoes and juices, beans, onions, broth, garlic, chili powder, cumin, allspice, cinnamon and pepper, in slow cooker. Cover; cook 5½ to 6 hours on LOW or until chicken is cooked through and celery is tender.

Makes 6 servings

Mediterranean Lentil Soup

Middle Eastern Lamb and Bean Stew

 2 tablespoons olive oil
 1 lamb shank (1 to 1½ pounds)
 4 cups chicken broth
 5 cloves garlic, crushed
 8 peppercorns
 2 slices bacon, chopped
 2 pounds boneless lamb stew meat,
      dredged in ½ cup all-purpose flour
 ½ medium sweet onion, chopped
 2 carrots, sliced in ½-inch rounds
 2 to 3 stalks celery, sliced diagonally into
      1-inch slices
 2 cans (15 ounces each) cannellini beans,
      drained
 ¼ cup cornstarch or arrowroot mixed with
      ¼ cup water
   Salt and black pepper

1. Heat oil in large saucepan over medium-high heat. Add lamb shank and brown on all sides.

2. Place browned lamb shank in slow cooker. Add chicken broth, garlic and peppercorns; cover and cook on HIGH 2 hours.

3. Add bacon to same saucepan in which lamb shank was browned and cook until crisp. Add half of stew meat to pan and brown on all sides. Add browned stew meat to slow cooker. Add onion and remaining stew meat to saucepan and cook until meat is browned on all sides. (Add additional oil if necessary.) Place remaining browned meat mixture in slow cooker. Cover; cook on HIGH 3 hours more.

4. During last 30 minutes of cooking, add carrots, celery, beans, and stir in cornstarch mixture. Before serving, season with salt and pepper and garnish with chopped fresh parsley or other herbs.   *Makes 4 to 6 servings*

Navy Bean Bacon Chowder

 1½ cups dried navy beans, rinsed
  2 cups cold water
  6 slices thick-cut bacon
  1 medium carrot, cut lengthwise into
      halves, then cut into 1-inch pieces
  1 rib celery, chopped
  1 medium onion, chopped
  1 small turnip, cut into 1-inch pieces
  1 teaspoon dried Italian seasoning
 ⅛ teaspoon black pepper
  1 large can (46 ounces) reduced-sodium
      chicken broth
  1 cup milk

1. Soak beans overnight in cold water.

2. Cook bacon in medium skillet over medium heat. Drain and crumble. Drain beans and discard soaking liquid. Combine beans, bacon, carrot, celery, onion, turnip, Italian seasoning and pepper in slow cooker; mix slightly. Pour broth over top. Cover; cook on LOW 7½ to 9 hours or until beans are tender.

3. Ladle 2 cups of soup mixture into food processor or blender. Process until smooth; return to slow cooker. Add milk; cover and heat on HIGH 10 minutes or until heated through.
                    Makes 6 servings

Middle Eastern Lamb and Bean Stew

Creamy Slow Cooker Seafood Chowder

1 quart (4 cups) half & half
2 cans (14½ ounces each) whole white
    potatoes, drained and cubed
1 bag (16 ounces) frozen hash brown
    potatoes
2 cans (10¾ ounces) condensed cream of
    mushroom soup, undiluted
1 onion, minced
½ cup (1 stick) butter, diced
1 teaspoon salt
1 teaspoon pepper
5 cans (about 8 ounces each) whole
    oysters, drained and rinsed
2 cans (about 6 ounces each) minced
    clams
2 cans (about 4 ounces each) cocktail
    shrimp, drained and rinsed

1. Combine half & half, canned and frozen potatoes, soup, onion, butter, salt and pepper in slow cooker. Mix very well.

2. Add oysters, clams and shrimp; stir gently.

3. Cover; cook on LOW for 4 to 5 hours.

Makes 8 to 10 servings

Chicken and Wild Rice Soup

3 cans (14½ ounces each) chicken broth
1 pound boneless skinless chicken breasts
    or thighs, cut into bite-size pieces
1 package (6 ounces) converted long grain
    and wild rice mix with seasoning
    packet (not quick-cooking or instant
    rice)
2 cups water
1 cup sliced celery
1 cup diced carrots
½ cup chopped onion
1 tablespoon dried parsley flakes
½ teaspoon black pepper

Combine all ingredients in slow cooker; mix well. Cover; cook on LOW 6 to 7 hours or on HIGH 4 to 5 hours.   *Makes 9 (1½ cups) servings*

Creamy Slow Cooker Seafood Chowder

Chicken and Wild Rice Soup

French Onion Soup

4 tablespoons butter, divided
3 pounds yellow onions, sliced
1 tablespoon sugar
2 to 3 tablespoons dry white wine or
   water (optional)
2 quarts (8 cups) beef broth
8 to 16 slices French bread
½ cup shredded Gruyère or Swiss cheese

1. Melt butter in large skillet over medium to low heat. Add onions; cover and cook just until onions are limp and transparent, but not browned, about 10 minutes.

2. Remove cover. Sprinkle sugar over onions. Cook, stirring, until onions are caramelized, 8 to 10 minutes. Scrape onions and any browned bits into slow cooker. If desired, deglaze pan by adding wine to pan, returning to heat, bringing to a boil and scraping up any browned bits with a wooden spoon. Add wine to slow cooker with onions. Stir in broth. Cover; cook on HIGH 6 hours or on LOW 8 hours.

3. Preheat broiler. To serve, ladle soup into individual soup bowls; top with 1 or 2 slices bread and about 1 tablespoon cheese. Place under broiler until cheese is melted and bubbly.

Makes 8 servings

Variation: Substitute 2 cups dry white wine for 2 cups of beef broth.

Easy Vegetarian Vegetable Bean Soup

3 cans (14 ounces each) vegetable broth
2 cups cubed unpeeled potatoes
2 cups sliced leeks, white part only (about
   3 medium)
1 can (14½ ounces) diced tomatoes,
   undrained
1 medium onion, chopped
1 cup chopped or shredded cabbage
1 cup sliced celery
1 cup sliced peeled carrots
3 cloves garlic, chopped
⅛ teaspoon dried rosemary
1 can (16 ounces) white beans, drained
   Salt and black pepper

1. Combine all ingredients except beans, salt and pepper in slow cooker. Cover; cook on LOW 8 hours.

2. Stir in beans and season with salt and pepper. Cover; cook about 30 minutes or until beans are heated through.

Makes 10 servings

Easy Does It

To thoroughly clean leeks, remove the root end and slice from top to bottom. Rinse under cold running water, separating the layers of leek to remove the dirt that collects there.

Easy Vegetarian Vegetable Bean Soup

Nancy's Chicken Noodle Soup

1 large can (48 ounces) chicken broth
2 boneless skinless chicken breasts, cut
   into bite-size pieces
4 cups water
2/3 cup diced onion
2/3 cup diced celery
2/3 cup diced carrots
2/3 cup sliced mushroom
1/2 cup frozen peas
4 chicken bouillon cubes
2 tablespoons margarine
1 tablespoon parsley flakes
1 teaspoon salt
1 teaspoon ground cumin
1 teaspoon dried marjoram leaves
1 teaspoon black pepper
2 cups cooked egg noodles

1. Combine all ingredients except noodles in slow cooker.

2. Cover; cook on LOW 4 to 6 hours or on HIGH for 3 to 4 hours, adding noodles one half hour before serving.   *Makes 4 servings*

French-Style Pork Stew

1 tablespoon vegetable oil
1 pork tenderloin (16 ounces), cut into
   3/4- to 1-inch cubes
1 medium onion, coarsely chopped
1 rib celery, sliced
1/2 teaspoon dried basil leaves
1/4 teaspoon dried rosemary, crushed
1/4 teaspoon dried oregano leaves
1 cup chicken broth
2 tablespoons all-purpose flour
1/2 package frozen mixed vegetables (about
   8 ounces), thawed
1 jar (4 1/2 ounces) sliced mushrooms,
   drained
1 package (about 6 ounces) long grain and
   wild rice
2 teaspoons lemon juice
1/8 teaspoon ground nutmeg
   Salt and black pepper

1. Heat oil in large skillet over high heat. Add pork, onion, celery, basil, rosemary and oregano. Cook until pork is browned. Place pork mixture in slow cooker. Stir chicken broth into flour until smooth; pour into slow cooker.

2. Stir in vegetables and mushrooms. Cover; cook on LOW 4 hours or until pork is barely pink in center. Prepare rice according to package directions, discarding spice packet, if desired.

3. Stir lemon juice and nutmeg into slow cooker. Season to taste with salt and pepper. Cover; cook 15 minutes. Serve stew over rice.
                                        Makes 4 servings

Nancy's Chicken Noodle Soup

Butternut Squash-Apple Soup

- **3 packages (12 ounces each) frozen cooked winter squash, thawed and drained** *or* **about 4½ cups mashed cooked butternut squash**
- **2 cans (14½ ounces each) chicken broth (3 to 4 cups)**
- **1 medium Golden Delicious apple, peeled and chopped**
- **2 tablespoons minced onion**
- **1 tablespoon packed light brown sugar**
- **1 teaspoon minced fresh sage** *or* **½ teaspoon ground sage**
- **¼ teaspoon ground ginger**
- **½ cup heavy cream or half & half**

1. Combine all ingredients except cream in slow cooker. Cover; cook on HIGH about 3 hours or on LOW about 6 hours.

2. Purée soup in blender, food processor or with electric mixer. Stir in cream just before serving.

Makes 6 to 8 servings

Note: For thicker soup, use 3 cups chicken broth.

Pasta Fagioli Soup

- **2 cans (14½ ounces each) reduced-sodium beef broth**
- **1 can (16 ounces) Great Northern beans, rinsed and drained**
- **1 can (14½ ounces) diced tomatoes, undrained**
- **2 medium zucchini, quartered lengthwise and sliced**
- **1 tablespoon olive oil**
- **1½ teaspoons minced garlic**
- **½ teaspoon dried basil leaves**
- **½ teaspoon dried oregano leaves**
- **½ cup tubetti, ditilini or small shell pasta, uncooked**
- **½ cup garlic seasoned croutons**
- **½ cup grated Asiago or Romano cheese**
- **3 tablespoons chopped fresh basil or Italian parsley (optional)**

1. Combine broth, beans, tomatoes with juice, zucchini, oil, garlic, dried basil and oregano in slow cooker; mix well. Cover; cook on LOW 3 to 4 hours.

2. Stir in pasta. Cover; continue cooking on LOW 1 hour or until pasta is tender.

3. Serve soup with croutons and cheese. Garnish with fresh basil, if desired.

Makes 5 to 6 servings

Butternut Squash-Apple Soup

Pasta Fagioli Soup

Lamb Stew

1 large sweet onion, chopped
2½ to 3½ tablespoons bacon fat or olive oil, divided
½ cup all-purpose flour
2 teaspoons salt
1 teaspoon black pepper
3 pounds boneless lamb for stew, cut into 2- to 2½-inch pieces
2 tablespoons sugar, divided
3 cans (14½ ounces each) beef broth
3 tablespoons tomato paste
4 cloves garlic, chopped
1 tablespoon dried thyme
1 tablespoon fresh chopped rosemary
2 bay leaves
1 pound carrots, peeled and cut into 2-inch chunks
1 pound petite Yukon gold potatoes, halved
1 package (10 ounces) frozen peas

1. Cook and stir onion in ½ tablespoon bacon fat in large skillet over medium heat until golden. Add to slow cooker.

2. Mix flour with salt and pepper in large bowl. Dredge lamb in flour mixture. Heat 1 tablespoon bacon fat in skillet over medium-high heat until hot. Add half of lamb to skillet and cook until browned on all sides. Add 1 tablespoon sugar and mix well to coat all of meat. Cook several minutes, until meat is caramelized. Add meat to slow cooker. Dredge and brown remaining lamb, using 1 to 2 tablespoons bacon fat as needed and remaining 1 tablespoon sugar.

3. Add broth to skillet and boil over high heat, scraping sides and bottom of pan to loosen browned bits. Add tomato paste, garlic, thyme, rosemary and bay leaves. Stir to combine. Pour over meat mixture in slow cooker. Cover; cook on LOW 4 hours or on HIGH 2 hours.

4. Add carrots and potatoes. Cover; cook 3 to 4 hours more on LOW or 1½ to 2½ hours on HIGH until vegetables and lamb are tender.

5. Add peas. Cook 30 minutes more.
Makes 6 to 8 servings

Three Bean Mole Chili

1 can (15 ounces) pinto beans, rinsed and drained
1 can (15 ounces) chili beans in spicy sauce, undrained
1 can (15 ounces) black beans, rinsed and drained
1 can (14½ ounces) Mexican or chili-style diced tomatoes, undrained
1 large green bell pepper, diced
1 small onion, diced
½ cup beef, chicken or vegetable broth
¼ cup prepared mole paste*
2 teaspoons ground cumin
2 teaspoons chili powder
2 teaspoons minced garlic
2 teaspoons ground coriander (optional)
Toppings: crushed tortilla chips, chopped cilantro or shredded cheese (optional)

Mole paste is available in the Mexican section of large supermarkets or in specialty markets.

1. Combine all ingredients except toppings in slow cooker; mix well. Cover; cook on LOW 5 to 6 hours or until vegetables are tender.

2. Serve with toppings, if desired.
Makes 4 to 6 servings

Three Bean Mole Chili

Italian Beef and Barley Soup

1 boneless beef top sirloin steak (about 1½ pounds)
1 tablespoon vegetable oil
4 medium carrots or parsnips, sliced ¼-inch thick
1 cup chopped onion
1 teaspoon dried thyme leaves
½ teaspoon dried rosemary
¼ teaspoon black pepper
⅓ cup pearl barley
2 cans (14½ ounces each) beef broth
1 can (14½ ounces) diced tomatoes with Italian seasoning, undrained

1. Cut beef into 1-inch pieces. Heat oil over medium-high heat in large skillet and brown beef on all sides. Set aside.

2. Place carrots and onion in slow cooker; sprinkle with thyme, rosemary and pepper. Top with barley and meat. Pour broth and tomatoes with juice over meat. Cover; cook on LOW 8 to 10 hours. *Makes 6 servings*

Easy Does It

Herbs and spices can lose their flavor with long slow cooking, so be sure to taste and adjust seasonings near the end of cooking time. Finishing the dish with a sprinkling of fresh herbs adds a nice touch of color, too.

Savory Bean Stew

1 cup frozen vegetable blend (onions, celery, red and green bell peppers)
1 can (15½ ounces) chick-peas (garbanzo beans), rinsed and drained
1 can (15 ounces) pinto beans, rinsed and drained
1 can (15 ounces) black beans, rinsed and drained
1 can (14½ ounces) diced tomatoes with roasted garlic, undrained
¾ teaspoon dried thyme leaves
¾ teaspoon dried sage leaves
½ to ¾ teaspoon dried oregano leaves
1 tablespoon all-purpose flour
¾ cup vegetable or chicken broth, divided

Polenta
3 cups water
¾ cup yellow cornmeal
¾ teaspoon salt
Additional salt and black pepper

1. Combine vegetable blend, chick-peas, beans, tomatoes and herbs in slow cooker. Blend flour with ½ cup vegetable broth; pour into bean mixture and stir well. Cover; cook on LOW 4 hours or until vegetables are tender and juice is thickened.

2. Meanwhile, prepare polenta. Bring 3 cups water to a boil in large saucepan. Reduce heat; gradually stir in cornmeal and salt. Cook 15 to 20 minutes or until cornmeal thickens. Season to taste with additional salt and pepper. Keep warm.

3. Stir remaining ¼ cup broth into slow cooker. Spread polenta on plate and top with stew. *Makes 6 (1-cup) servings*

Italian Beef and Barley Soup

Roast Tomato-Basil Soup

**2 cans (28 ounces each) peeled whole
tomatoes, drained, seeded and liquid
reserved
2½ tablespoons packed dark brown sugar
1 medium onion, finely chopped
3 cups tomato liquid reserved from
canned tomatoes
3 cups chicken broth
3 tablespoons tomato paste
¼ teaspoon ground allspice
1 can (5 ounces) evaporated milk
¼ cup shredded fresh basil leaves (about
10 large)
Salt and black pepper**

1. To roast tomatoes, preheat oven to 450°F.
Line cookie sheet with foil; spray with nonstick
cooking spray. Arrange tomatoes on foil in single
layer. Sprinkle with brown sugar and top with
onion. Bake about 25 to 30 minutes or until
tomatoes look dry and light brown. Let tomatoes
cool slightly; finely chop.

2. Place tomato mixture, 3 cups reserved liquid,
chicken broth, tomato paste and allspice in slow
cooker. Mix well. Cover; cook on LOW 8 hours
or on HIGH 4 hours.

3. Add evaporated milk and basil; season with
salt and pepper. Cook 30 minutes or until hot.
Garnish as desired.   *Makes 6 servings*

Potato and Leek Soup

**4 cups chicken broth
3 potatoes, peeled and diced
1½ cups chopped cabbage
1 leek, diced
1 onion, chopped
2 carrots, diced
¼ cup chopped fresh parsley
1 teaspoon salt
½ teaspoon caraway seeds
½ teaspoon black pepper
1 bay leaf
½ cup sour cream
1 pound bacon, cooked and crumbled**

Combine chicken broth, potatoes, cabbage, leek,
onion, carrots and parsley in large bowl; pour
mixture into slow cooker. Stir in salt, caraway
seeds, pepper and bay leaf. Cover; cook on
LOW 8 to 10 hours or on HIGH 4 to 5 hours.
Remove and discard bay leaf. Combine some
hot liquid from slow cooker with sour cream in
small bowl. Add mixture to slow cooker; stir. Stir
in bacon.   *Makes 6 to 8 servings*

Roast Tomato-Basil Soup

Potato and Leek Soup

No-Chop Black Bean Soup

3 cans (15 ounces each) black beans,
  rinsed and drained
1 package (12 ounces) frozen diced green
  bell peppers
2 cups frozen chopped onion
2 cans (14½ ounces each) fat-free or
  regular chicken broth
1 can (14½ ounces) diced tomatoes with
  pepper, celery and onion, undrained
1 teaspoon bottled minced garlic
1½ teaspoons ground cumin, divided
¾ teaspoon salt
2 tablespoons extra virgin olive oil

In slow cooker, combine beans, bell peppers,
onion, broth, tomatoes, garlic and 1 teaspoon of
cumin. Cover; cook on HIGH 5 hours or on LOW
8 to 10 hours. Just before serving, stir in salt,
remaining ½ teaspoon cumin and oil.

Makes 8 servings

Sausage, Butter Bean and Cabbage Soup

2 tablespoons butter, divided
1 large onion, chopped
12 ounces smoked sausage such as
  kielbasa or andouille, cut into ½-inch
  slices
8 cups chicken broth
½ Savoy cabbage, coarsely shredded
3 tablespoons tomato paste
1 bay leaf
4 medium tomatoes, chopped
2 cans (14 ounces each) butter beans,
  drained
Salt and black pepper

1. Melt 1 tablespoon butter in large skillet over medium heat. Add onion; cook and stir 3 to 4 minutes or until golden. Place in slow cooker.

2. Melt remaining 1 tablespoon butter in the same skillet; cook sausage until brown on both sides. Add to slow cooker.

3. Place chicken broth, cabbage, tomato paste and bay leaf in slow cooker; stir until well blended. Cover; cook on LOW 4 hours or HIGH 2 hours.

4. Add tomatoes and beans; season with salt and pepper. Cover; cook 1 hour until heated through. Remove and discard bay leaf.

Makes 6 servings

Easy Does It

The waxy-leaved, compact head of green cabbage is the easiest to find and the most familiar kind of cabbage. The lesser-known Savoy cabbage is worth seeking out for its milder, sweeter flavor. Savoy cabbage has a loose, full head of very crinkled, dark to pale green leaves. These two cabbage varieties may be used interchangeably.

No-Chop Black Bean Soup

Chinese Chicken Stew

- **1 pound boneless skinless chicken thighs, cut into 1-inch pieces**
- **1 teaspoon Chinese five-spice powder***
- **½ to ¾ teaspoon red pepper flakes**
- **1 tablespoon peanut or vegetable oil**
- **1 large onion, coarsely chopped**
- **1 package (8 ounces) fresh mushrooms, sliced**
- **2 cloves garlic, minced**
- **1 can (about 14 ounces) chicken broth, divided**
- **1 tablespoon cornstarch**
- **1 large red bell pepper, cut into ¾-inch pieces**
- **2 tablespoons soy sauce**
- **2 large green onions, cut into ½-inch pieces**
- **1 tablespoon sesame oil**
- **3 cups hot cooked white rice (optional)**
- **¼ cup coarsely chopped fresh cilantro (optional)**

Chinese five-spice powder is a blend of cinnamon, cloves, fennel seed, anise seed and Szechuan peppercorns. It is available in some large supermarkets and specialty stores.

1. Toss chicken with five-spice powder in small bowl. Season with red pepper flakes. Heat peanut oil in large skillet. Add onion and chicken; cook and stir about 5 minutes or until chicken is browned. Add mushrooms and garlic; cook and stir until chicken is no longer pink.

2. Combine ¼ cup broth and cornstarch in small bowl; set aside. Place cooked chicken mixture, remaining broth, red bell pepper and soy sauce in slow cooker. Cover; cook on LOW 3½ hours or until peppers are tender.

3. Stir in cornstarch mixture, green onions and sesame oil; cook 30 to 45 minutes or until juices have thickened. Ladle into soup bowls; scoop ½ cup rice into each bowl and sprinkle with cilantro, if desired.   *Makes 6 servings*

Peppery Potato Soup

- **2 cans (14½ ounces each) chicken broth**
- **4 small baking potatoes, halved and sliced**
- **1 large onion, quartered and sliced**
- **1 rib celery with leaves, sliced**
- **¼ cup all-purpose flour**
- **¾ teaspoon black pepper**
- **½ teaspoon salt**
- **1 cup half & half**
- **1 tablespoon butter**
  Celery leaves or fresh parsley

1. Combine broth, potatoes, onion, celery, flour, pepper and salt in slow cooker; mix well. Cover; cook on LOW 6 to 7½ hours.

2. Stir in half & half; cover and continue to cook 1 hour.

3. Remove slow cooker lid. Slightly crush potato mixture with potato masher. Continue to cook, uncovered, an additional 30 minutes until slightly thickened. Just before serving, stir in butter. Garnish with celery leaves, if desired.
   Makes 6 (1¼-cup) servings

Peppery Potato Soup

Beef Stew

- **3 pounds beef for stew, cut in 1½-inch cubes**
- **5 carrots, cut into bite-size pieces**
- **5 potatoes, diced**
- **4 onions, quartered**
- **2 stalks celery, chopped**
- **1 can (about 28 ounces) diced tomatoes, undrained**
- **1½ cups water**
- **1½ tablespoons salt**
- **1½ teaspoons paprika**
- **1½ teaspoons Worcestershire sauce**
- **¾ teaspoon black pepper**
- **1 clove garlic, minced**
- **1 bay leaf**

1. Place meat, carrots, potatoes, onion, celery and tomatoes with juices in slow cooker. Blend water with spices in medium bowl. Add to slow cooker; stir to combine.

2. Cover; cook on LOW 10 to 12 hours. Stir occasionally.   *Makes 8 servings*

Simmering Hot & Sour Soup

- **2 cans (14½ ounces each) chicken broth**
- **1 cup chopped cooked chicken or pork**
- **4 ounces fresh shiitake mushroom caps, thinly sliced**
- **½ cup sliced bamboo shoots, cut into thin strips**
- **3 tablespoons rice or rice wine vinegar**
- **2 tablespoons soy sauce**
- **1½ teaspoons chili paste *or* 1 teaspoon hot chili oil**
- **4 ounces firm tofu, well drained and cut into ½-inch pieces**
- **2 teaspoons Asian sesame oil**
- **2 tablespoons cornstarch**
- **2 tablespoons cold water**
- **Chopped cilantro or sliced green onions**

1. Combine chicken broth, chicken, mushrooms, bamboo shoots, vinegar, soy sauce and chili paste in slow cooker. Cover; cook on LOW for 3 to 4 hours.

2. Stir in tofu and sesame oil. Combine cornstarch with water; mix well. Stir into soup. Cover; cook on HIGH 10 minutes or until soup is thickened.

3. Serve hot; garnish with cilantro.
Makes 4 servings

Beef Stew

Simmering Hot & Sour Soup

Fiesta Black Bean Soup

6 cups chicken broth
¾ pound potatoes, peeled and diced
1 can (16 ounces) black beans, drained
½ pound ham, diced
½ onion, diced
1 can (4 ounces) chopped jalapeño
    peppers*
2 cloves garlic, minced
2 teaspoons dried oregano leaves
1½ teaspoons dried thyme leaves
1 teaspoon ground cumin
    Sour cream, chopped bell peppers and
    chopped tomatoes for garnish
    (optional)

Jalapeño peppers can sting and irritate the skin; wear rubber gloves when handling peppers and do not touch eyes. Wash hands after handling.

Combine all ingredients, except garnish, in slow cooker. Cover; cook on LOW 8 to 10 hours or on HIGH 4 to 5 hours until vegetables are tender. Garnish, if desired.   *Makes 6 to 8 servings*

Simmered Split Pea Soup

3 cans (14½ ounces each) chicken broth
1 package (16 ounces) dry split peas
1 medium onion, diced
2 medium carrots, diced
1 teaspoon black pepper
½ teaspoon dried thyme leaves
1 bay leaf
8 slices bacon, crisp-cooked and crumbled,
    divided

1. Place broth, split peas, onion, carrots, pepper, thyme, bay leaf and half of crumbled bacon in slow cooker.

2. Cover; cook on LOW 6 to 8 hours or until vegetables are tender. Remove and discard bay leaf and adjust seasonings. Garnish with remaining bacon.   *Makes 6 servings*

Beer and Cheese Soup

2 to 3 slices pumpernickel or rye bread
1 can (about 14 ounces each) chicken
    broth
1 cup beer
¼ cup finely chopped onion
2 cloves garlic, minced
¾ teaspoon dried thyme leaves
6 ounces American cheese, shredded or
    diced
4 to 6 ounces sharp Cheddar cheese,
    shredded
1 cup milk
½ teaspoon paprika
    Croutons (optional)

1. Preheat oven to 425°F. Slice bread into ½-inch cubes; place on baking sheet. Bake 10 to 12 minutes, stirring once, or until crisp; set aside.

2. Combine chicken broth, beer, onion, garlic and thyme in slow cooker. Cover; cook on LOW 4 hours. Turn to HIGH. Stir cheeses, milk and paprika into slow cooker. Cook 45 to 60 minutes or until soup is hot and cheeses are melted. Stir soup well to blend cheeses. Ladle soup into bowls; top with croutons, if desired.
     Makes 4 (1-cup) servings

Fiesta Black Bean Soup

Turkey Vegetable Chili Mac

Nonstick cooking spray
¾ pound ground turkey breast
1 can (about 15 ounces) black beans,
**   rinsed and drained**
1 can (14½ ounces) Mexican-style diced
**   tomatoes, undrained**
1 can (14½ ounces) no-salt-added diced
**   tomatoes, undrained**
1 cup frozen corn
½ cup chopped onion
2 cloves garlic, minced
1 teaspoon Mexican seasoning
½ cup uncooked elbow macaroni
⅓ cup sour cream

1. Spray large skillet with nonstick cooking spray.
Add turkey; cook until browned. Combine
cooked turkey, beans, tomatoes, corn, onion,
garlic and seasoning in slow cooker. Cover; cook
on LOW 4 to 5 hours.

2. Stir in macaroni. Cover and cook 10 minutes;
stir. Cover; cook 20 to 30 minutes more or until
pasta is tender. Serve with sour cream.

Makes 6 servings

Minestrone alla Milanese

2 cans (14½ ounces each) reduced-sodium
**   beef broth**
1 can (14½ ounces) diced tomatoes,
**   undrained**
1 cup diced potato
1 cup coarsely chopped green cabbage
1 cup coarsely chopped carrots
1 cup sliced zucchini
¾ cup chopped onion
¾ cup sliced fresh green beans
¾ cup coarsely chopped celery
¾ cup water
2 tablespoons olive oil
1 clove garlic, minced
½ teaspoon dried basil leaves
¼ teaspoon dried rosemary
1 bay leaf
1 can (15½ ounces) cannellini beans,
**   rinsed and drained**
Grated Parmesan cheese (optional)

Combine all ingredients except cannellini beans
and cheese in slow cooker; mix well. Cover;
cook on LOW 5 to 6 hours. Add cannellini
beans. Cover; cook on LOW 1 hour or until
vegetables are crisp-tender. Remove and discard
bay leaf. Garnish with cheese, if desired.

Makes 8 to 10 servings

Minestrone alla Milanese

Savory Pea Soup with Sausage

8 ounces smoked sausage, cut lengthwise into halves, then cut into ½-inch pieces
1 package (16 ounces) dried split peas, sorted and rinsed
3 medium carrots, sliced
2 ribs celery, sliced
1 medium onion, chopped
¾ teaspoon dried marjoram leaves
1 bay leaf
2 cans (14½ ounces each) reduced-sodium chicken broth

1. Heat small skillet over medium heat. Add sausage; cook 5 to 8 minutes or until browned. Drain well.

2. Combine sausage and remaining ingredients in slow cooker. Cover; cook on LOW 4 to 5 hours or until peas are tender. Turn off heat. Remove and discard bay leaf. Cover and let stand 15 minutes to thicken. *Makes 6 servings*

Easy Italian Vegetable Soup

1 can (14½ ounces) diced tomatoes, undrained
1 can (10½ ounces) condensed beef broth
1 package (8 ounces) sliced mushrooms
1 medium yellow onion, chopped
1 medium zucchini, thinly sliced
1 medium green bell pepper, chopped
⅓ cup dry red wine or beef broth
1½ tablespoons dried basil leaves
2½ teaspoons sugar
1 tablespoon extra virgin olive oil
½ teaspoon salt
1 cup (4 ounces) shredded Mozzarella cheese (optional)

1. Combine tomatoes, broth, mushrooms, onion, zucchini, bell pepper, wine, basil and sugar in slow cooker. Cover; cook on LOW 8 hours or on HIGH 4 hours.

2. Stir oil and salt into soup. Serve garnished with cheese, if desired. *Makes 5 to 6 servings*

Savory Pea Soup with Sausage

Easy Italian Vegetable Soup

Rustic Vegetable Soup

1 jar (16 ounces) picante sauce
**1 package (10 ounces) frozen mixed
    vegetables, thawed**
**1 package (10 ounces) frozen cut green
    beans, thawed**
**1 can (10 ounces) condensed beef broth,
    undiluted**
**1 to 2 baking potatoes, cut into ½-inch
    pieces**
1 medium green bell pepper, chopped
½ teaspoon sugar
¼ cup finely chopped fresh parsley

Combine all ingredients except parsley in slow cooker. Cover; cook on LOW 8 hours or on HIGH 4 hours. Stir in parsley; serve.

Makes 8 servings

Potato-Crab Chowder

1 package (10 ounces) frozen corn
1 cup frozen hash brown potatoes
¾ cup finely chopped carrots
1 teaspoon dried thyme leaves
¾ teaspoon garlic-pepper seasoning
**3 cups fat-free reduced-sodium chicken
    broth**
½ cup water
1 cup evaporated milk
3 tablespoons cornstarch
1 can (6 ounces) crabmeat, drained
½ cup sliced green onions

1. Place corn, potatoes and carrots in slow cooker. Sprinkle with thyme and garlic-pepper seasoning. Add broth and water. Cover; cook on LOW 3½ to 4½ hours.

2. Stir together evaporated milk and cornstarch in medium bowl. Stir into slow cooker. Cover; cook on HIGH 1 hour. Just before serving, stir in crabmeat and green onions. Garnish as desired.

Makes 5 servings

Beef Fajita Soup

1 pound beef for stew
**1 can (15 ounces) pinto beans, rinsed and
    drained**
**1 can (15 ounces) black beans, rinsed and
    drained**
**1 can (14½ ounces) diced tomatoes with
    roasted garlic, undrained**
1 can (14 ounces) beef broth
1½ cups water
1 small green bell pepper, thinly sliced
1 small red bell pepper, thinly sliced
1 small onion, thinly sliced
2 teaspoons ground cumin
1 teaspoon seasoned salt
1 teaspoon black pepper
    **Toppings: sour cream, shredded
        Monterey Jack or Cheddar cheese,
        chopped olives (optional)**

1. Combine all ingredients in slow cooker except Toppings.

2. Cover; cook on LOW 8 hours or until beef is tender.

3. Serve topped with sour cream, shredded Monterey Jack or Cheddar cheese and chopped olives, if desired.

Makes 8 servings

Beef Fajita Soup

Farmhouse Ham and Vegetable Chowder

**2 cans (10½ ounces each) condensed
    cream of celery soup
2 cups diced cooked ham
1 package (10 ounces) frozen corn
1 large baking potato, cut into ½-inch
    pieces
1 medium red bell pepper, diced
½ teaspoon dried thyme leaves
2 cups small broccoli florets
½ cup milk**

1. Combine all ingredients except broccoli and milk in slow cooker; stir to blend. Cover; cook on LOW 6 to 8 hours or on HIGH 3 to 4 hours.

2. If cooking on LOW, turn to HIGH; stir in broccoli and milk. Cover; cook 15 minutes or until broccoli is crisp tender.   *Makes 6 servings*

Tortilla Soup

**2 cans (14½ ounces each) chicken broth
1 can (14½ ounces) diced tomatoes with
    jalapeño peppers, undrained
2 cups chopped carrots
2 cups frozen whole kernel corn
1½ cups chopped onion
1 can (8 ounces) tomato sauce
1 tablespoon chili powder
1 teaspoon ground cumin
¼ teaspoon garlic powder
2 cups chopped cooked chicken (optional)
    Shredded Monterey Jack cheese
    Tortilla chips, broken**

1. Combine broth, tomatoes with juice, carrots, corn, onion, tomato sauce, chili powder, cumin and garlic powder in slow cooker. Cover; cook on LOW 6 to 8 hours.

2. Stir in chicken, if desired. Ladle into bowls. Top each serving with cheese and tortilla chips.
Makes 6 servings

Vegetable Medley Soup

**3 sweet potatoes, peeled and chopped
3 zucchini, chopped
2 cups chopped broccoli
1 onion, chopped
¼ cup butter, melted
3 cans (about 14 ounces each) chicken
    broth
2 white potatoes, peeled and shredded
1 rib celery, finely chopped
1 tablespoon salt
1 teaspoon ground cumin
1 teaspoon black pepper
2 cups half & half or milk**

1. Combine sweet potatoes, zucchini, broccoli, onion and butter in large bowl. Add chicken broth; stir. Add white potatoes, celery, salt, cumin and pepper; stir. Pour mixture into slow cooker.

2. Cover; cook on LOW 8 to 10 hours or on HIGH 4 to 5 hours. Add half & half; cook 30 minutes to 1 hour or until heated through.
Makes 12 servings

Vegetable Medley Soup

The Vegetable Patch

From Vegetarian Sausage

Rice to Orange-Spiced

Sweet Potatoes, these

recipes prove that slow is

the way to go for meatless

main courses and stunning

sides. The slow cooker

makes it so easy, you don't

even have to boil water!

Vegetarian Sausage Rice

2 cups chopped green bell peppers
1 can (15½ ounces) dark kidney beans,
  rinsed and drained
1 can (14½ ounces) diced tomatoes with
  green bell peppers and onions,
  undrained
1 cup chopped onion
1 cup sliced celery
1 cup water, divided
¾ cup uncooked long-grain white rice
1¼ teaspoons salt
1 teaspoon hot pepper sauce
½ teaspoon dried thyme leaves
½ teaspoon red pepper flakes
3 bay leaves
1 package (8-ounces) vegetable protein
  breakfast patties, thawed
2 tablespoons extra virgin olive oil
½ cup chopped fresh parsley
  Additional hot pepper sauce (optional)

1. Combine bell peppers, beans, tomatoes with juice, onion, celery, ½ cup water, rice, salt, thyme, pepper flakes and bay leaves in slow cooker. Cover; cook on LOW 4 to 5 hours. Remove bay leaves.

2. Dice breakfast patties. Heat oil in large nonstick skillet over medium-high heat. Add patties; cook 2 minutes or until lightly browned, scraping bottom of skillet occasionally.

3. Place patties in slow cooker. *Do not stir.* Add remaining ½ cup water to skillet; bring to a boil over high heat 1 minute, scraping up bits on bottom of skillet. Add liquid and parsley to slow cooker; stir gently to blend. Serve immediately with additional hot pepper sauce, if desired.

Makes 8 cups

Vegetarian Sausage Rice

Cornbread and Bean Casserole

Filling

1 medium onion, chopped
1 medium green bell pepper, diced
2 cloves garlic, minced
1 can (16 ounces) red kidney beans, rinsed and drained
1 can (16 ounces) pinto beans, rinsed and drained
1 can (16 ounces) diced tomatoes with jalapeño peppers, undrained
1 can (8 ounces) tomato sauce
1 teaspoon chili powder
½ teaspoon ground cumin
½ teaspoon black pepper
¼ teaspoon hot pepper sauce

Topping

1 cup yellow cornmeal
1 cup all-purpose flour
2½ teaspoons baking powder
1 tablespoon sugar
½ teaspoon salt
1¼ cups milk
2 eggs
3 tablespoons vegetable oil
1 can (8½ ounces) cream-style corn, undrained

1. Lightly grease slow cooker. Cook onion, bell pepper and garlic in large skillet over medium heat until tender. Transfer to slow cooker. Stir in kidney beans, pinto beans, tomatoes with juice, tomato sauce, chili powder, cumin, black pepper and hot pepper sauce. Cover; cook on HIGH 1 hour.

2. Combine cornmeal, flour, baking powder, sugar and salt in large bowl. Stir in milk, eggs and oil; mix well. Stir in corn. Spoon evenly over bean mixture. Cover; cook on HIGH 1½ to 2 hours or until cornbread topping is done.

Makes 6 to 8 servings

Note: Spoon any remaining cornbread topping into greased muffin cups; bake at 375°F 30 minutes or until golden brown.

Asparagus and Cheese Side Dish

1½ pounds fresh asparagus, trimmed
2 cups crushed saltine crackers
1 can (10¾ ounces) condensed cream of asparagus soup, undiluted
1 can (10¾ ounces) condensed cream of chicken soup, undiluted
⅔ cup slivered almonds
¼ pound American cheese, cut into cubes
1 egg

Combine all ingredients in large bowl; stir well. Pour into slow cooker. Cover; cook on HIGH 3 to 3½ hours.

Makes 4 to 6 servings

Asparagus and Cheese Side Dish

Orange-Spice Glazed Carrots

1 package (32 ounces) baby carrots
½ cup packed light brown sugar
½ cup orange juice
3 tablespoons butter or margarine
¾ teaspoon ground cinnamon
¼ teaspoon ground nutmeg
¼ cup cold water
2 tablespoons cornstarch

Combine all ingredients except cornstarch and water in slow cooker. Cover; cook on LOW 3½ to 4 hours or until carrots are crisp-tender. Spoon carrots into serving bowl. Remove juices to small saucepan. Heat to a boil. Mix water and cornstarch in small bowl until blended. Stir into saucepan. Boil 1 minute or until thickened, stirring constantly. Spoon over carrots.

Makes 6 servings

Peasant Potatoes

4 tablespoons unsalted butter
1 large sweet onion, chopped
2 large cloves garlic, chopped
1 teaspoon dried oregano
½ pound smoked beef sausage, cut into ¾-inch slices
6 medium potatoes, preferably Yukon Gold, cut into 1½- to 2-inch pieces
Salt and pepper
2 cups sliced Savoy or other cabbage
1 cup diced or sliced roasted red bell pepper
½ cup shaved fresh Parmesan cheese

1. In large skillet over medium heat, melt butter. Add onion and garlic. Cook and stir 5 minutes or until onion is transparent. Stir in oregano and sausage and cook 5 minutes more. Stir in potatoes, salt and pepper until well mixed. Transfer mixture to slow cooker.

2. Cover; cook on HIGH 3 to 4 hours or on LOW 6 to 8 hours, stirring every hour if possible. During last 30 minutes of cooking, add cabbage and peppers.

3. Sprinkle with Parmesan cheese before serving.

Makes 6 side-dish servings

Orange-Spice Glazed Carrots

Peasant Potatoes

Red Cabbage and Apples

- 1 small head red cabbage, cored and thinly sliced
- 3 medium apples, peeled and grated
- ¾ cup sugar
- ½ cup red wine vinegar
- 1 teaspoon ground cloves
- 1 cup crisp-cooked and crumbled bacon (optional)

Combine cabbage, apples, sugar, red wine vinegar and cloves in slow cooker. Cover; cook on HIGH 6 hours, stirring after 3 hours. Sprinkle with bacon, if desired. *Makes 4 to 6 servings*

Risi Bisi

- 1½ cups converted long-grain white rice
- ¾ cup chopped onion
- 2 cloves garlic, minced
- 2 cans (about 14 ounces each) reduced-sodium chicken broth
- ⅓ cup water
- ¾ teaspoon dried Italian seasoning
- ½ teaspoon dried basil leaves
- ½ cup frozen peas, thawed
- ¼ cup grated Parmesan cheese
- ¼ cup toasted pine nuts (optional)

1. Combine rice, onion and garlic in slow cooker. Heat broth and water in small saucepan to a boil. Stir boiling liquid, Italian seasoning and basil into rice mixture. Cover; cook on LOW 2 to 3 hours or until liquid is absorbed.

2. Add peas. Cover; cook 1 hour. Stir in cheese. Spoon rice into serving bowl. Sprinkle with pine nuts, if desired. *Makes 6 servings*

Escalloped Corn

- 2 tablespoons butter or margarine
- ½ cup chopped onion
- 3 tablespoons all-purpose flour
- 1 cup milk
- 4 cups frozen corn, thawed, divided
- ½ teaspoon salt
- ½ teaspoon dried thyme leaves
- ¼ teaspoon black pepper
- ⅛ teaspoon ground nutmeg
- Fresh thyme (optional)

1. Heat butter in small saucepan over medium heat. Add onion; cook and stir 5 minutes or until tender. Add flour. Cook over medium heat 1 minute, stirring constantly. Stir in milk and heat to a boil. Boil 1 minute or until thickened, stirring constantly.

2. Process half the corn in food processor or blender until coarsely chopped. Combine milk mixture, processed and whole corn, salt, dried thyme, pepper and nutmeg in slow cooker. Cover; cook on LOW 3½ to 4 hours or until mixture is bubbly around edge. Garnish with fresh thyme, if desired. *Makes 6 servings*

Variation: Add ½ cup (2 ounces) shredded Cheddar cheese and 2 tablespoons grated Parmesan cheese before serving. Stir until melted. Garnish with additional shredded Cheddar cheese, if desired.

Red Cabbage and Apples

Donna's Potato Casserole

1 can (10¾ ounces) condensed cream of
  chicken soup, undiluted
8 ounces sour cream
¼ cup chopped onion
¼ cup plus 3 tablespoons butter, melted,
  divided
1 teaspoon salt
2 pounds potatoes, peeled and chopped
2 cups (8 ounces) shredded Cheddar
  cheese
1½ to 2 cups stuffing mix

1. Combine soup, sour cream, onion, ¼ cup
butter and salt in small bowl.

2. Combine potatoes and cheese in slow
cooker. Pour soup mixture into slow cooker; mix
well. Sprinkle stuffing mix over potato mixture;
drizzle with remaining 3 tablespoons butter.
Cover; cook on LOW 8 to 10 hours or on HIGH
5 to 6 hours or until potatoes are tender.

Makes 8 to 10 servings

Southwestern Stuffed Peppers

4 green bell peppers
1 can (16 ounces) black beans, rinsed and
  drained
1 cup (4 ounces) shredded Pepper-Jack
  cheese
¾ cup medium salsa
½ cup frozen corn
½ cup chopped green onions with tops
⅓ cup uncooked long grain converted rice
1 teaspoon chili powder
½ teaspoon ground cumin
  Sour cream (optional)

1. Cut thin slice off top of each bell pepper.
Carefully remove seeds, leaving pepper whole.

2. Combine remaining ingredients except sour
cream in medium bowl. Spoon filling evenly into
each pepper. Place peppers in slow cooker.
Cover; cook on LOW 4 to 6 hours. Serve with
dollop of sour cream, if desired.

Makes 4 servings

Easy Does It

Store potatoes in a cool, dark, dry, well-ventilated place. Do not refrigerate them. It is important to protect potatoes from light, which can cause them to turn green and loose quality.

Southwestern Stuffed Peppers

Spicy Beans Tex-Mex

⅓ **cup lentils**
1⅓ **cups water**
5 **strips bacon**
1 **onion, chopped**
1 **can (16 ounces) pinto beans, undrained**
1 **can (16 ounces) red kidney beans,**
   undrained
1 **can (15 ounces) diced tomatoes,**
   undrained
3 **tablespoons ketchup**
3 **cloves garlic, minced**
1 **teaspoon chili powder**
½ **teaspoon ground cumin**
¼ **teaspoon red pepper flakes**
1 **bay leaf**

1. Boil lentils in water 20 to 30 minutes in large saucepan; drain. In small skillet, cook bacon until crisp; remove, drain and crumble bacon. In same skillet, cook onion in bacon drippings until soft.

2. Combine lentils, bacon, onion, beans with juice, tomatoes with juice, ketchup, garlic, chili powder, cumin, pepper flakes and bay leaf in slow cooker. Cook on HIGH 3 to 4 hours. Remove bay leaf before serving.

Makes 8 to 10 servings

Orange-Spiced Sweet Potatoes

2 **pounds sweet potatoes, peeled and**
   diced
½ **cup dark brown sugar, packed**
½ **cup butter (1 stick), cut into small pieces**
1 **teaspoon ground cinnamon**
½ **teaspoon ground nutmeg**
½ **teaspoon orange zest**
   Juice of 1 medium orange
¼ **teaspoon salt**
1 **teaspoon vanilla**
   Chopped, toasted pecans

Place all ingredients, except pecans, in slow cooker. Cover; cook on HIGH 2 hours or on LOW 4 hours or until potatoes are tender. Sprinkle with pecans before serving.

Makes 8 (½-cup) servings

Variation: Mash potatoes with a hand masher or electric mixer; add ¼ cup milk or cream for a moister consistency. Sprinkle with a cinnamon-sugar mixture.

Spicy Beans Tex-Mex

Orange-Spiced Sweet Potatoes

Three Pepper Pasta Sauce

2 cans (14½ ounces each) diced tomatoes,
    undrained
1 *each* red, yellow and green bell pepper,
    cut into 1-inch pieces
1 cup chopped onion
1 can (6 ounces) tomato paste
4 cloves garlic, minced
2 tablespoons olive oil
1 teaspoon dried basil leaves
1 teaspoon dried oregano leaves
½ teaspoon salt
¼ teaspoon red pepper flakes or ground
    black pepper
    Hot cooked pasta
    Shredded Parmesan or Romano cheese

1. Combine all ingredients except pasta and cheese in slow cooker. Cover; cook on LOW 7 to 8 hours or until vegetables are tender.

2. Adjust seasonings, if desired. Serve with pasta and cheese.   *Makes 4 to 6 servings*

Substitution: 3 cups mixed bell pepper chunks from a salad bar may be substituted for peppers.

Sweet & Hot Onion Relish

3 cups chopped onion
½ cup mild salsa
½ cup packed dark brown sugar
1 tablespoon cider vinegar
¼ to ½ teaspoon red pepper flakes

1. Combine all ingredients in slow cooker. Cover; cook on LOW 7 to 8 hours or on HIGH 3 to 4 hours until onions are very tender.

2. Serve at room temperature as a condiment for roast pork or chicken or chilled over cream cheese.   *Makes 1½ cups relish*

Bean Pot Medley

1 can (15½ ounces) black beans, rinsed
    and drained
1 can (15½ ounces) red beans, rinsed and
    drained
1 can (15½ ounces) Great Northern beans,
    rinsed and drained
1 can (15½ ounces) black-eyed peas, rinsed
    and drained
1 can (8½ ounces) baby lima beans, rinsed
    and drained
1½ cups ketchup
1 cup chopped onion
1 cup chopped red bell pepper
1 cup chopped green bell pepper
½ cup packed brown sugar
½ cup water
2 to 3 teaspoons cider vinegar
1 teaspoon dry mustard
2 bay leaves
⅛ teaspoon black pepper

Combine all ingredients in slow cooker; stir. Cover; cook on LOW 6 to 7 hours or until onion and bell peppers are tender. Remove and discard bay leaves.   *Makes 8 servings*

Three Pepper Pasta Sauce

Layered Mexican-Style Casserole

- 2 cans (15½ ounces each) hominy*, drained
- 1 can (15 ounces) black beans, rinsed and drained
- 1 can (14½ ounces) diced tomatoes with garlic, basil and oregano, undrained
- 1 cup thick and chunky salsa
- 1 can (6 ounces) tomato paste
- ½ teaspoon ground cumin
- 3 large (about 9-inch diameter) flour tortillas
- 2 cups (8 ounces) shredded Monterey Jack cheese
- ¼ cup sliced black olives

Hominy is corn that has been treated with slaked lime to remove the germ and hull. It can be found with the canned vegetables in most supermarkets.

1. Spray slow cooker with nonstick cooking spray. Prepare foil handles to make removing tortilla stack easier. Crisscross three 18x2-inch strips of heavy duty foil in a spoke design in slow cooker.

2. Stir together hominy, beans, tomatoes with juice, salsa, tomato paste and cumin in large bowl. Press one tortilla in bottom of slow cooker. (Edges of tortilla may turn up slightly.) Top with one third of hominy mixture and one third of cheese. Repeat layers. Press remaining tortilla on top. Top with remaining hominy mixture. Set aside remaining cheese.

3. Cover; cook on LOW 6 to 8 hours. Sprinkle with remaining cheese and olives. Cover; let stand 5 minutes. Pull out tortilla stack with foil handles.   *Makes 6 servings*

Middle Eastern Vegetable Stew

- 1 tablespoon olive oil
- 3 cups (12 ounces) sliced zucchini
- 2 cups (6 ounces) cubed peeled eggplant
- 2 cups (8 ounces) sliced quartered sweet potatoes
- 1½ cups cubed peeled butternut squash
- 1 can (28 ounces) crushed tomatoes in purée
- 1 cup drained chick-peas (garbanzo beans)
- ½ cup raisins or currants
- 1½ teaspoons ground cinnamon
- 1 teaspoon grated orange peel
- ¾ to 1 teaspoon ground cumin
- ½ teaspoon salt
- ½ teaspoon paprika
- ¼ to ½ teaspoon ground red pepper
- ⅛ teaspoon ground cardamom
  Hot cooked rice or couscous (optional)

Combine all ingredients except rice in slow cooker. Cover; cook on LOW 5 to 5½ hours or until vegetables are tender. Serve over rice, if desired.   *Makes 4 to 6 servings*

Layered Mexican-Style Casserole

Spanish Paella-Style Rice

2 cans (14½ ounces each) chicken broth
1½ cups converted long grain rice,
    uncooked (not quick cooking or
    instant rice)
1 small red bell pepper, diced
⅓ cup dry white wine or water
½ teaspoon powdered saffron *or*
    ½ teaspoon turmeric
⅛ teaspoon red pepper flakes
½ cup frozen peas, thawed
    Salt

1. Combine broth, rice, bell pepper, wine, saffron and pepper flakes in slow cooker; mix well. Cover; cook on LOW 4 hours or until liquid is absorbed.

2. Stir in peas. Cover; cook on LOW 15 to 30 minutes or until peas are hot. Season with salt.   *Makes 6 servings*

Note: Paella is a Spanish dish of saffron-flavored rice combined with a variety of meats, seafood and vegetables. Paella is traditionally served in a wide, shallow dish.

Winter Squash and Apples

1 teaspoon salt
½ teaspoon black pepper
1 butternut squash (about 2 pounds),
    peeled and seeded
2 apples, cored and cut into slices
1 medium onion, quartered and sliced
1½ tablespoons butter

1. Combine salt and pepper in small bowl; set aside.

2. Cut squash into 2-inch pieces and place into slow cooker. Add apples and onion. Sprinkle with salt mixture; stir well. Cover; cook on LOW 6 to 7 hours.

3. Just before serving, stir in butter and season with additional salt and pepper to taste.
                    Makes 4 to 6 servings

Variation: Add ¼ to ½ cup brown sugar and ½ teaspoon cinnamon with butter; mix well.

Spanish Paella-Style Rice

Winter Squash and Apples

Rustic Cheddar Mashed Potatoes

2 pounds russet potatoes, peeled and diced
1 cup water
⅓ cup butter, cut in small pieces
½ to ¾ cup milk
1¼ teaspoons salt
½ teaspoon black pepper
½ cup finely chopped green onions
2 to 3 ounces shredded Cheddar cheese

1. Combine potatoes and water in slow cooker; dot with butter. Cover; cook on HIGH 3 hours or on LOW 6 hours or until potatoes are tender.

2. Using an electric mixer on medium setting, whip potatoes until well blended. Add milk, salt and pepper; whip until well blended. Stir in green onions and cheese, cover tightly and let stand 15 minutes to allow flavors to blend and cheese to melt.   *Makes 8 servings*

Bean and Vegetable Burritos

2 tablespoons chili powder
2 teaspoons dried oregano leaves
1½ teaspoons ground cumin
1 large sweet potato, peeled and diced
1 can black beans or pinto beans, rinsed and drained
4 cloves garlic, minced
1 medium onion, halved and thinly sliced
1 jalapeño pepper,* seeded and minced
1 green bell pepper, chopped
1 cup frozen corn, thawed and drained
3 tablespoons lime juice
1 tablespoon chopped fresh cilantro
¾ cup (3 ounces) shredded Monterey Jack cheese
4 (10-inch) flour tortillas
Sour cream (optional)

*Jalapeño peppers can sting and irritate the skin; wear rubber gloves when handling peppers and do not touch eyes. Wash hands after handling.

1. Combine chili powder, oregano and cumin in small bowl. Set aside.

2. Layer ingredients in slow cooker in the following order: sweet potato, beans, half of chili powder mix, garlic, onion, jalapeño pepper, bell pepper, remaining half of chili powder mix and corn. Cover; cook on LOW 5 hours or until sweet potato is tender. Stir in lime juice and cilantro.

3. Preheat oven to 350°F. Spoon 2 tablespoons cheese in center of each tortilla. Top with 1 cup filling. Fold all 4 sides to enclose filling. Place burritos seam side down on baking sheet. Cover with foil and bake 20 to 30 minutes or until heated through. Serve with sour cream, if desired.   *Makes 4 servings*

Rustic Cheddar Mashed Potatoes

Vegetarian Lasagna

1 small eggplant, sliced into ½-inch rounds
½ teaspoon salt
2 tablespoons olive oil, divided
1 tablespoon butter
½ pound mushrooms, sliced
1 small onion, diced
1 can (26 ounces) pasta sauce
1 teaspoon dried basil
1 teaspoon dried oregano
2 cups part-skim ricotta cheese
1½ cups shredded Monterey Jack cheese
1 cup grated Parmesan cheese, divided
1 package (8 ounces) whole wheat
**   lasagna, cooked and drained**
1 medium zucchini, thinly sliced

1. Sprinkle eggplant with salt; let sit 10 to 15 minutes. Rinse and pat dry, then brush with 1 tablespoon olive oil. Brown on both sides in medium skillet over medium heat. Set aside.

2. Heat remaining 1 tablespoon olive oil and butter in same skillet over medium heat; cook and stir mushrooms and onions until softened. Stir in pasta sauce, basil and oregano. Set aside.

3. In medium bowl, mix together ricotta cheese, Monterey Jack cheese and ½ cup Parmesan cheese. Set aside.

4. Spread ⅓ sauce mixture in bottom of slow cooker. Layer with ⅓ of lasagna noodles, ½ of eggplant, ½ of cheese mixture. Repeat layers once. For last layer, use final ⅓ of lasagna noodles, zucchini, final ⅓ of sauce mixture and top with remaining ½ cup Parmesan.

5. Cover; cook on LOW 6 hours. Let sit 15 to 20 minutes before serving.   *Makes 4 servings*

Pesto Rice and Beans

1 can (15 ounces) Great Northern beans,
**   rinsed and drained**
1 can (14 ounces) chicken broth
¾ cup uncooked long-grain white rice
1½ cups frozen cut green beans, thawed
**   and drained**
½ cup prepared pesto
**   Grated Parmesan cheese (optional)**

1. Combine Great Northern beans, chicken broth and rice in slow cooker. Cover; cook on LOW 2 hours.

2. Stir in green beans; cover and cook 1 hour or until rice and beans are tender. Turn off slow cooker and remove insert to heatproof surface. Stir in pesto and Parmesan cheese, if desired. Let stand, covered, 5 minutes or until cheese is melted. Serve immediately.   *Makes 8 servings*

Easy Does It

It's hard to see inside a slow cooker once the lid is covered with condensation, but don't lift the lid to peek which drastically lowers the temperature. Instead, just spin the cover until the condensation falls off.

Vegetarian Lasagna

Scalloped Potatoes and Parsnips

6 tablespoons unsalted butter
3 tablespoons all-purpose flour
1¾ cups heavy cream
2 teaspoons dry mustard
1½ teaspoons salt
1 teaspoon dried thyme leaves
½ teaspoon black pepper
2 baking potatoes, cut in half lengthwise,
**   then in ¼-inch slices crosswise**
2 parsnips, cut into ¼-inch slices
1 onion, chopped
2 cups (8 ounces) shredded sharp Cheddar
**   cheese**

1. Melt butter in medium saucepan over medium-high heat. Add flour and whisk constantly 3 to 5 minutes. Slowly whisk in cream, mustard, salt, thyme and pepper. Stir until smooth.

2. Place potatoes, parsnips and onion into slow cooker. Add cream sauce. Cover; cook on LOW 7 hours or on HIGH 3½ hours or until potatoes are tender. Stir in cheese. Cover until cheese melts. *Makes 4 to 6 servings*

Spinach Spoonbread

1 package (10 ounces) frozen chopped
**   spinach, thawed and squeezed dry**
1 red bell pepper, diced
4 eggs, lightly beaten
1 cup cottage cheese
1 package (5½ ounces) cornbread mix
6 green onions, sliced
½ cup butter, melted
1¼ teaspoons seasoned salt

1. Lightly grease slow cooker; preheat on HIGH.

2. Combine all ingredients in large bowl; mix well. Pour batter into preheated slow cooker. Cook, covered with lid slightly ajar to allow excess moisture to escape, on HIGH 1 hour 45 minutes to 2 hours or on LOW 3 to 4 hours or until edges are golden and knife inserted in center of bread comes out clean.

3. Serve bread spooned from slow cooker, or loosen edges and bottom with knife and invert onto plate. Cut into wedges to serve. *Makes 8 servings*

Scalloped Potatoes and Parsnips

Spinach Spoonbread

Risotto-Style Peppered Rice

1 cup uncooked converted long grain rice
1 medium green bell pepper, chopped
1 medium red bell pepper, chopped
1 cup chopped onion
½ teaspoon ground turmeric
⅛ teaspoon ground red pepper (optional)
1 can (14½ ounces) fat-free chicken broth
4 ounces Monterey Jack cheese with
    jalapeño peppers, cubed
½ cup milk
¼ cup (½ stick) butter, cubed
1 teaspoon salt

1. Place rice, bell peppers, onion, turmeric and red pepper, if desired, into slow cooker. Stir in broth. Cover; cook on LOW 4 to 5 hours or until rice is done.

2. Stir in cheese, milk, butter and salt; fluff rice with fork. Cover; cook on LOW 5 minutes or until cheese melts.   *Makes 4 to 6 servings*

Polenta-Style Corn Casserole

1 can (14½ ounces) chicken broth
½ cup cornmeal
1 can (7 ounces) corn, drained
1 can (4 ounces) green chilies, drained
¼ cup diced red bell pepper
½ teaspoon salt
¼ teaspoon black pepper
1 cup shredded Cheddar cheese

1. Pour chicken broth into slow cooker. Whisk in cornmeal. Add corn, chilies, bell pepper, salt and pepper. Cover; cook on LOW 4 to 5 hours or on HIGH 2 to 3 hours.

2. Stir in cheese. Continue cooking, uncovered, 15 to 30 minutes or until cheese melts.
Makes 6 servings

Serving Suggestion: Divide cooked corn mixture into lightly greased individual ramekins or spread in pie plate; cover and refrigerate. Serve at room temperature or warm in oven or microwave.

Meatless Sloppy Joes

2 cups thinly sliced onions
2 cups chopped green peppers
1 can (about 15 ounces) kidney beans,
    drained and mashed
1 can (8 ounces) tomato sauce
2 tablespoons ketchup
1 tablespoon mustard
2 cloves garlic, finely chopped
1 teaspoon chili powder
    Cider vinegar (optional)
2 sandwich rolls, halved

Combine all ingredients except vinegar and rolls in slow cooker. Cover; cook on LOW 5 to 5½ hours or until vegetables are tender. Season to taste with cider vinegar, if desired. Serve on rolls.   *Makes 4 servings*

Risotto-Style Peppered Rice

Mediterranean Red Potatoes

**3 medium red potatoes, cut in half
  lengthwise, then crosswise into pieces
⅔ cup fresh or frozen pearl onions
  Nonstick garlic-flavored cooking spray
¾ teaspoon dried Italian seasoning
¼ teaspoon black pepper
1 small tomato, seeded and chopped
2 ounces (½ cup) feta cheese, crumbled
2 tablespoons chopped black olives**

1. Place potatoes and onions in 1½-quart soufflé dish. Spray potatoes and onions with cooking spray; toss to coat. Add Italian seasoning and pepper; mix well. Cover dish tightly with foil.

2. Tear off 3 (18×3-inch) strips of heavy-duty aluminum foil. Cross strips to resemble wheel spokes. Place soufflé dish in center of strips. Pull foil strips up and over dish and place dish into slow cooker.

3. Pour hot water into slow cooker to about 1½ inches from top of soufflé dish. Cover; cook on LOW 7 to 8 hours.

4. Use foil handles to lift dish out of slow cooker. Stir tomato, feta cheese and olives into potato mixture. *Makes 4 servings*

Vegetable Pasta Sauce

**2 cans (14½ ounces each) diced tomatoes,
  undrained
1 can (14½ ounces) whole tomatoes,
  undrained
1½ cups sliced mushrooms
1 medium red bell pepper, diced
1 medium green bell pepper, diced
1 small yellow squash, cut into ¼-inch
  slices
1 small zucchini, cut into ¼-inch slices
1 can (6 ounces) tomato paste
4 green onions, sliced
2 tablespoons dried Italian seasoning
1 tablespoon chopped fresh parsley
3 cloves garlic, minced
1 teaspoon salt
1 teaspoon red pepper flakes (optional)
1 teaspoon black pepper
  Hot cooked pasta
  Parmesan cheese and fresh basil for
    garnish (optional)**

Combine all ingredients except pasta and garnishes in slow cooker, stirring until well blended. Cover; cook on LOW 6 to 8 hours. Serve over cooked pasta. Garnish with Parmesan cheese and fresh basil, if desired.
Makes 4 to 6 servings

Mediterranean Red Potatoes

Green Bean Casserole

2 packages (10 ounces each) frozen green
    beans, thawed
1 can (10½ ounces) condensed cream of
    mushroom soup
1 tablespoon chopped fresh parsley
1 tablespoon chopped roasted red peppers
1 teaspoon dried sage leaves
½ teaspoon salt
½ teaspoon black pepper
¼ teaspoon ground nutmeg
½ cup toasted slivered almonds

Combine all ingredients except almonds in slow
cooker. Cover; cook on LOW 3 to 4 hours.
Sprinkle with almonds.   *Makes 4 to 6 servings*

Green Bean Casserole

Cran-Orange Acorn Squash

3 small acorn squash
5 tablespoons instant brown rice
3 tablespoons minced onion
3 tablespoons diced celery
3 tablespoons dried cranberries
    Pinch ground or dried sage
1 teaspoon butter, cut into bits
3 tablespoons orange juice
½ cup water

1. Slice off tops of squash and enough of squash
bottom, so it will sit upright. Scoop out seeds
and discard; set squash aside.

2. Combine rice, onion, celery, cranberries and
sage in small bowl. Stuff squash with rice
mixture; dot with butter. Pour 1 tablespoon
orange juice into each squash over stuffing.
Stand squash in slow cooker. Pour water into
bottom of slow cooker.

3. Cover; cook on LOW 2½ hours or until
squash is tender.   *Makes 6 servings*

Tip: The skin of squash can defy even the
sharpest knives. To make slicing easier,
microwave the whole squash at HIGH 5 minutes
to soften the skin.

Cran-Orange Acorn Squash

Cheesy Broccoli Casserole

**2 packages (10 ounces each) chopped
   broccoli, thawed
1 can (10¾ ounces) condensed cream of
   potato soup
1¼ cups (5 ounces) shredded sharp Cheddar
   cheese, divided
¼ cup minced onions
1 teaspoon hot pepper sauce
1 cup crushed saltine crackers or potato
   chips**

1. Lightly grease slow cooker. Combine broccoli, soup, 1 cup cheese, onions and pepper sauce in slow cooker; mix thoroughly. Cover; cook on LOW 5 to 6 hours or on HIGH 2½ to 3 hours.

2. Uncover; sprinkle top with crackers and remaining ½ cup cheese. Cook, uncovered, on LOW 30 to 60 minutes or until cheese melts.

Makes 4 to 6 servings

Note: If desired, casserole may be spooned into a baking dish and garnished with additional cheese and crackers; bake 5 to 10 minutes in preheated 400°F oven.

Swiss Cheese Scalloped Potatoes

**2 pounds baking potatoes, peeled and
   thinly sliced
½ cup finely chopped yellow onion
¼ teaspoon salt
¼ teaspoon ground nutmeg
2 tablespoons butter, cut into small pieces
½ cup milk
2 tablespoons all-purpose flour
3 ounces Swiss cheese slices, torn into
   small pieces
¼ cup finely chopped green onions
   (optional)**

1. Layer ½ of potatoes, ¼ cup onion, ⅛ teaspoon salt, ⅛ teaspoon nutmeg and 1 tablespoon butter in slow cooker. Repeat layers. Cover; cook on LOW 7 hours or on HIGH 4 hours. Remove potatoes with slotted spoon to serving dish and keep warm.

2. Blend milk and flour in small bowl until smooth. Stir mixture into slow cooker. Add cheese; stir to combine. If slow cooker is on LOW, turn to HIGH. Cover; cook until slightly thickened, about 10 minutes. Stir. Pour cheese mixture over potatoes and serve. Garnish with chopped green onions, if desired.

Makes 5 to 6 servings

Cheesy Broccoli Casserole

Beefed Up Dinners

Tender is the word for slow-cooked beef. Even less expensive cuts like short ribs or brisket will yield to a fork. Better yet, what used to be only-on-Sunday pot roast is now a weeknight possibility with the help of a slow cooker.

Braciola

1 can (28 ounces) tomato sauce
2½ teaspoons dried oregano leaves, divided
1¼ teaspoons dried basil leaves, divided
1 teaspoon salt
½ pound bulk hot Italian sausage
½ cup chopped onion
¼ cup grated Parmesan cheese
2 cloves garlic, minced
1 tablespoon dried parsley flakes
1 to 2 beef flank steaks (about 2½ pounds)

1. Combine tomato sauce, 2 teaspoons oregano, 1 teaspoon basil and salt in medium bowl; set aside.

2. Cook sausage in large nonstick skillet over medium-high heat until no longer pink stirring to separate; drain well. Combine sausage, onion, cheese, garlic, parsley, remaining ½ teaspoon oregano and ¼ teaspoon basil in medium bowl; set aside.

3. Place steak on countertop between two pieces waxed paper. Pound with meat mallet until steak is ⅛ to ¼ inch thick. Cut steak into about 3-inch wide strips.

4. Spoon sausage mixture evenly onto each strip. Roll up jelly-roll style, securing meat with toothpicks. Place each roll in slow cooker. Pour reserved tomato sauce mixture over meat. Cover; cook on LOW 6 to 8 hours.

5. Cut each roll into slices. Arrange slices on dinner plates. Top with hot tomato sauce.

Makes 6 to 8 servings

Braciola

Campbell's® Savory Pot Roast

1 can (10¾ ounces) CAMPBELL'S®
    Condensed Cream of Mushroom Soup
    or 98% Fat Free Cream of Mushroom
    Soup
1 pouch CAMPBELL'S® Dry Onion Soup
    and Recipe Mix
6 medium potatoes, cut into 1-inch pieces
    (about 6 cups)
6 medium carrots, thickly sliced (about
    3 cups)
1 (3½- to 4-pound) boneless chuck pot
    roast, trimmed

In slow cooker mix soup, soup mix, potatoes
and carrots. Add roast and turn to coat. Cover
and cook on **low** 8 to 9 hours or until roast and
vegetables are done.   *Makes 7 to 8 servings*

Easy Does It

**To make a smooth sauce in a
slow cooker, use condensed soup
or evaporated milk. Fresh dairy
products, if used, should only be
added near the end of the
cooking time or you risk them
separating.**

Slow-Cooked Korean Beef Short Ribs

4 to 4½ pounds beef short ribs
¼ cup chopped green onions with tops
¼ cup tamari or soy sauce
¼ cup beef broth or water
1 tablespoon brown sugar
2 teaspoons minced fresh ginger
2 teaspoons minced garlic
½ teaspoon black pepper
2 teaspoons Asian sesame oil
    Hot cooked rice or linguini pasta
2 teaspoons sesame seeds, toasted

1. Place ribs in slow cooker. Combine green
onions, soy sauce, broth, brown sugar, ginger,
garlic and pepper in medium bowl; mix well and
pour over ribs. Cover; cook on LOW 7 to 8 hours
or until ribs are fork tender.

2. Remove ribs from cooking liquid, cool slightly.
Trim excess fat. Cut rib meat into bite-sized
pieces discarding bones and fat.

3. Let cooking liquid stand 5 minutes to allow
fat to rise. Skim off fat.

4. Stir sesame oil into liquid. Return beef to
slow cooker. Cover; cook on LOW 15 to
30 minutes or until mixture is hot.

5. Serve with rice or pasta; garnish with sesame
seeds.   *Makes 6 servings*

Variation: 3 pounds boneless short ribs may be
substituted for bone-in short ribs.

Slow-Cooked Korean Beef Short Ribs

Mexican-Style Shredded Beef

1 beef chuck shoulder roast (about 3 pounds)
1 tablespoon chili powder
1 tablespoon ground cumin
1 tablespoon ground coriander
1 teaspoon salt
½ teaspoon ground red pepper
1 cup salsa or picante sauce
2 tablespoons water
1 tablespoon cornstarch

1. Cut roast in half. Combine chili powder, cumin, coriander, salt and red pepper in small bowl. Rub over beef. Place ¼ cup of salsa in slow cooker; top with one piece beef. Layer ¼ cup salsa, remaining beef and ½ cup salsa in slow cooker. Cover; cook on LOW 8 to 10 hours or until meat is tender.

2. Remove beef from cooking liquid; cool slightly. Trim and discard excess fat from beef. Using two forks, shred meat.

3. Let cooking liquid stand 5 minutes to allow fat to rise. Skim off fat. To thicken liquid blend water and cornstarch. Whisk into liquid. Cook on HIGH until thickened. Return beef to slow cooker and cook 15 to 30 minutes until hot. Adjust seasonings, if desired.

4. Serve as meat filling for tacos, fajitas or burritos. Leftover mixture may be refrigerated up to 3 days or frozen up to 3 months.

Makes 5 cups filling

Curry Beef

1 pound lean ground beef
1 medium onion, thinly sliced
½ cup beef broth
1 tablespoon curry powder
1 teaspoon ground cumin
2 cloves garlic, minced
1 cup (8 ounces) sour cream
¼ cup reduced-fat (2%) milk
½ cup raisins, divided
1 teaspoon sugar
12 ounces wide egg noodles or 1⅓ cups long-grain white rice
¼ cup chopped walnuts, almonds or pecans

1. Heat large skillet over high heat. Add beef, cook until browned; pour off fat.

2. Add onion, beef broth, curry powder, cumin, garlic and cooked beef to slow cooker. Cover; cook on LOW 4 hours. Stir in sour cream, milk, ¼ cup raisins and sugar. Cover; cook 30 minutes or until thickened and heated through.

3. Cook noodles according to package directions; drain. Spoon beef curry over noodles. Sprinkle with remaining ¼ cup raisins and walnuts.   *Makes 4 servings*

Serving Suggestion: Serve with sliced cucumber sprinkled with sugar and vinegar or plain yogurt topped with brown sugar, chopped bananas and green onions.

Mexican-Style Shredded Beef

The Best Beef Stew

½ cup plus 2 tablespoons all-purpose flour, divided
2 teaspoons salt
1 teaspoon black pepper
3 pounds beef for stew, cut into 1-inch pieces
1 can (16 ounces) diced tomatoes in juice, undrained
3 potatoes, peeled and diced
½ pound smoked sausage, sliced
1 cup chopped leek
1 cup chopped onion
4 ribs celery, sliced
½ cup chicken broth
3 cloves garlic, minced
1 teaspoon dried thyme leaves
3 tablespoons water

1. Combine ½ cup flour, salt and pepper in resealable plastic food storage bag. Add beef; shake bag to coat beef. Place beef in slow cooker. Add remaining ingredients except remaining 2 tablespoons flour and water; stir well. Cover; cook on LOW 8 to 12 hours or on HIGH 4 to 6 hours.

2. One hour before serving, turn slow cooker to HIGH. Combine remaining 2 tablespoons flour and water in small bowl; stir until mixture becomes paste. Stir mixture into slow cooker; mix well. Cover and cook until thickened. Garnish as desired.   *Makes 8 servings*

Sloppy Sloppy Joes

4 pounds ground beef
1 cup chopped onion
1 cup chopped green bell pepper
1 can (about 28 ounces) tomato sauce
2 cans (10¾ ounces each) condensed tomato soup, undiluted
1 cup packed brown sugar
¼ cup ketchup
3 tablespoons Worcestershire sauce
1 tablespoon dry mustard
1 tablespoon prepared mustard
1½ teaspoons chili powder
1 teaspoon garlic powder

1. Cook beef in large skillet over medium-high heat until no longer pink, stirring to break up meat. Drain fat. Add onion and green pepper and cook, stirring frequently, 5 to 10 minutes or until onion becomes translucent and mixture becomes fragrant.

2. Transfer meat mixture to slow cooker. Add remaining ingredients; stir well to combine.

3. Cover; cook on LOW 4 to 6 hours.
    Makes 20 to 25 servings

The Best Beef Stew

Sloppy Sloppy Joe

Mom's Spaghetti Sauce

7½ cups water
3 cans (15 ounces each) tomato purée
3 cans (6 ounces each) tomato paste
1 can (14½ ounces) tomatoes, undrained
2 large onions, chopped
3 tablespoons sugar
2 tablespoons salt
1½ tablespoons Italian seasoning blend
1½ tablespoons dried oregano leaves
1 tablespoon black pepper
6 large garlic cloves, minced
3 bay leaves
2 to 2½ pounds Italian hot or sweet sausage (optional)
3 pounds ground beef, shaped into about 35 meatballs and browned (optional)

1. Add all ingredients, except optional sausage and meatballs, to slow cooker; mix well. If using optional sausage and meatballs, you will need to prepare sauce in two slow cookers.

2. Cover; cook on HIGH 1 hour. Add meatballs and sausages to each slow cooker, if desired. Cover; cook on LOW 6 to 8 hours.

Makes 10 to 12 servings

Tip: Serve over hot spaghetti or your favorite pasta. Any sauce leftover after the meat has been eaten can be served over cooked boneless, skinless chicken breasts or used to make a flavorful base for a pot of vegetable soup.

Texas-Style Barbecued Brisket

1 beef brisket (3 to 4 pounds)
3 tablespoons Worcestershire sauce
1 tablespoon chili powder
1 teaspoon celery salt
1 teaspoon black pepper
1 teaspoon liquid smoke
2 cloves garlic, minced
2 bay leaves
2 cups prepared barbecue sauce

1. Trim excess fat from meat and discard. Place meat in resealable plastic food storage bag. Combine Worcestershire sauce, chili powder, celery salt, pepper, liquid smoke, garlic and bay leaves in small bowl. Spread mixture on all sides of meat; seal bag. Refrigerate 24 hours.

2. Place meat and marinade in slow cooker. Cut in half to fit in slow cooker if necessary. Cover; cook on LOW 7 hours.

3. Remove meat from slow cooker and pour juices into 2-cup measure; let stand 5 minutes. Skim fat from juices. Remove and discard bay leaves. Stir 1 cup defatted juices into barbecue sauce. Discard remaining juices. Return meat and barbecue sauce to slow cooker. Cover; cook on LOW 1 hour or until meat is fork-tender. Remove meat to cutting board. Cut across grain into ¼-inch-thick slices. Serve 2 to 3 tablespoons barbecue sauce over each serving.

Makes 10 to 12 servings

Mom's Spaghetti Sauce

Cabbage Rolls

1 large head cabbage, cored
Salt
3 pounds ground beef
1 pound pork sausage
2 medium onions, chopped
1½ cups cooked rice
1 egg
2 tablespoons prepared horseradish
2 tablespoons ketchup
1 envelope (about 1 ounce) dry onion soup mix
1 tablespoon salt
1 teaspoon allspice
½ teaspoon garlic powder
Black pepper
Sauce for Cabbage Rolls (recipe follows)

1. In large stockpot filled halfway with salted water, place cabbage core-side down. Simmer over medium heat 5 minutes or until outside leaves come off easily. Continue to simmer and pull out rest of leaves. Set aside; reserve cabbage water.

2. Stir together remaining ingredients in large mixing bowl. Roll meat mixture into 3-inch balls. Place one meat ball into each cabbage leaf; roll up, fold in edges and secure with toothpick. Continue with remaining cabbage rolls.

3. Place cabbage rolls in slow cooker. Cover; cook on LOW 5 hours or until meat is cooked through and cabbage is tender. Serve with sauce poured over top of rolls.   *Makes 16 servings*

Sauce for Cabbage Rolls

3 cans (10¾ ounces each) condensed cheese soup, undiluted
2½ cups reserved cabbage water
1 can (10¾ ounces) condensed tomato soup, undiluted

Heat all ingredients in medium saucepan over medium heat until warm.

Campbell's® Asian Tomato Beef

2 cans (10¾ ounces each) CAMPBELL'S® Condensed Tomato Soup
⅓ cup soy sauce
⅓ cup vinegar
1½ teaspoons garlic powder
¼ teaspoon pepper
1 (3- to 3½-pound) boneless beef round steak, ¾ inch thick, cut into strips
6 cups broccoli flowerets
8 cups hot cooked rice

1. In slow cooker mix soup, soy sauce, vinegar, garlic powder, pepper and beef. Cover and cook on *low* 7 to 8 hours or until beef is done.

2. Stir. Arrange broccoli over beef. Cover and cook on *high* 15 minutes more or until tender-crisp. Serve over rice.   *Makes 8 servings*

Tip: No time to chop fresh produce? Buy bags of precut vegetables—they work great in many recipes!

Cabbage Rolls

Deviled Beef Short Rib Stew

4 pounds beef short ribs, trimmed
2 pounds small red potatoes, scrubbed
    and scored
8 carrots, peeled and cut into chunks
2 onions, cut into thick wedges
1 bottle (12 ounces) beer or non-alcoholic
    malt beverage
8 tablespoons *French's®* **Bold n' Spicy**
    Brown Mustard, divided
3 tablespoons *French's®* **Worcestershire**
    Sauce, divided
2 tablespoons cornstarch

1. Broil ribs 6 inches from heat on rack in broiler pan 10 minutes or until well browned, turning once. Place vegetables in bottom of slow cooker. Place ribs on top of vegetables.

2. Combine beer, *6 tablespoons* mustard and *2 tablespoons* Worcestershire in medium bowl. Pour into slow cooker. Cover and cook on high 5 hours* or until meat is tender.

3. Transfer meat and vegetables to platter; keep warm. Strain fat from broth; pour broth into saucepan. Combine cornstarch with *2 tablespoons cold water* in small bowl. Stir into broth with remaining *2 tablespoons* mustard and *1 tablespoon* Worcestershire. Heat to boiling. Reduce heat to medium-low. Cook 1 to 2 minutes or until thickened, stirring often. Pass gravy with meat and vegetables. Serve meat with additional mustard.

Makes 6 servings (with 3 cups gravy)

*Or cook 10 hours on low.

Tip: Prepare ingredients the night before for quick assembly in the morning. Keep refrigerated until ready to use.

Italian Beef

1 beef rump roast (3 to 5 pounds)
1 can (14 ounces) beef broth
2 cups mild giardiniera

1. Put rump roast in slow cooker and add beef broth and giardiniera.

2. Cover; cook on LOW 10 hours.

3. Shred and serve with sauce on crusty Italian rolls.

Makes 8 servings

Italian Beef

Deviled Beef Short Rib Stew

Fiery Chili Beef

1 beef flank steak (1 to 1½ pounds)
1 can (28 ounces) diced tomatoes, undrained
1 can (15 ounces) pinto beans, rinsed and drained
1 medium onion, chopped
2 cloves garlic, minced
½ teaspoon salt
½ teaspoon ground cumin
¼ teaspoon black pepper
1 canned chipotle chile pepper in adobo sauce
1 teaspoon adobo sauce from canned chile pepper
Flour tortillas

*Chipotle chili peppers are dried, smoked jalapeño peppers with a hot, yet sweet and smoky flavor. They are available in most supermarkets in the Mexican foods section canned in adobo sauce. Leftover chilies in adobo can be frozen for later use.

1. Cut flank steak in 6 evenly-sized pieces. Place flank steak, tomatoes with juice, beans, onion, garlic, salt, cumin and black pepper into slow cooker.

2. Dice chile pepper. Add pepper and adobo sauce to slow cooker; mix well. Cover; cook on LOW 7 to 8 hours. Serve with tortillas.

Makes 6 servings

Spanish-Style Couscous

1 pound lean ground beef
1 can (about 14 ounces) beef broth
1 small green bell pepper, cut into ½-inch pieces
½ cup pimiento-stuffed green olives, sliced
½ medium onion, chopped
2 cloves garlic, minced
1 teaspoon ground cumin
½ teaspoon dried thyme leaves
1⅓ cups water
1 cup uncooked couscous

1. Heat skillet over high heat until hot. Add beef; cook until browned. Pour off fat. Place broth, bell pepper, olives, onion, garlic, cumin, thyme and beef in slow cooker. Cover; cook on LOW 4 hours or until bell pepper is tender.

2. Bring water to a boil over high heat in small saucepan. Stir in couscous. Cover; remove from heat. Let stand 5 minutes; fluff with fork. Spoon couscous onto plates; top with beef mixture.

Makes 4 servings

Fiery Chili Beef

Shelby Slow Cooker Rouladen

12 slices top round beef, pounded thin (¼-inch thick)
Salt and pepper
Garlic pepper
4 tablespoons Dijon mustard
1½ cups chopped onion
1½ cups chopped dill pickle
4 tablespoons butter
5 tablespoons flour
2 cans (14½ ounces each) beef broth
1 pound peeled baby carrots
4 stalks celery, cut into 1-inch pieces

1. Place 1 slice of beef on clean cutting board, season with salt, pepper and garlic pepper. Spread with about 1 teaspoon of mustard and top with about ⅛ cup each onion and pickle. Starting at one short side of beef fold about ⅓ of slice over on itself, tuck in long sides, then roll tightly. Secure with toothpick. Repeat with remaining slices of beef.

2. Brown half of rolled beef slices in large skillet coated with nonstick cooking spray over medium-high heat. Once thoroughly browned on all sides, brown remaining rolls and remove.

3. In same skillet, melt butter. Sprinkle with flour, and stir to make smooth paste. Add beef broth, stirring constantly. Cook and stir until mixture thickens.

4. Pour half of gravy in slow cooker. Add beef rolls, and cover with remaining gravy. Top with carrots and celery.

5. Cover; cook on HIGH 4 to 5 hours or on LOW 8 to 10 hours. *Makes 6 to 8 servings*

Creamy Beef and Noodles

1 tablespoon vegetable oil
2 pounds beef for stew, cut into 1-inch pieces
1 jar (4 ounces) sliced mushrooms, drained
¼ cup minced onion
3 cloves garlic, minced
1 teaspoon salt
1 teaspoon black pepper
⅛ teaspoon dried thyme
1 bay leaf
1 can (14½ ounces) beef broth
⅓ cup cooking sherry
1 container (8 ounces) sour cream
½ cup all-purpose flour
¼ cup water
4 cups hot cooked noodles

1. Heat oil in large skillet over medium-high heat. Add beef; cook and stir until brown. Drain fat.

2. Place beef, mushrooms, onion, garlic, salt, pepper, thyme and bay leaf in slow cooker. Add beef broth and sherry. Cover and cook on LOW 8 to 10 hours. Remove and discard bay leaf.

3. Increase heat to HIGH. Combine sour cream, flour and water in small bowl. Stir about 1 cup of hot liquid into sour cream mixture. Stir mixture into slow cooker. Cover; cook on HIGH 30 minutes or until thickened and bubbly. Serve over noodles. *Makes 6 to 8 servings*

Shelby Slow Cooker Rouladen

Best Corned Beef Ever

1 to 2 beef briskets (about 5 pounds total)
2 cups apple cider, divided
1 head garlic, cloves separated, crushed and peeled
2 tablespoons whole peppercorns
2 tablespoons dried thyme leaves *or* **1 cup fresh thyme**
1 tablespoon mustard seed
1 tablespoon Cajun seasoning
1 teaspoon ground cumin
1 teaspoon celery seed
1 teaspoon ground allspice
2 to 4 whole cloves
1 bottle (12 ounces) dark beer

1. Place brisket, ⅓ cup cider, garlic, peppercorns, thyme, mustard seed, Cajun seasoning, cumin, celery seed, allspice and cloves in zip-top plastic bag to marinate. Seal and refrigerate overnight.

2. Place brisket and marinade in slow cooker. Add remaining 1½ cups apple cider and beer.

3. Cover; cook on LOW 10 hours. Strain sauce and pour over meat. *Makes 12 servings*

Yankee Pot Roast and Vegetables

1 beef chuck pot roast (2½ pounds)
 Salt and black pepper
3 medium baking potatoes (about 1 pound), unpeeled and cut into quarters
2 large carrots, cut into ¾-inch slices
2 ribs celery, cut into ¾-inch slices
1 medium onion, sliced
1 large parsnip, cut into ¾-inch slices
2 bay leaves
1 teaspoon dried rosemary
½ teaspoon dried thyme leaves
½ cup reduced-sodium beef broth
2 to 4 tablespoons flour

1. Trim excess fat from meat and discard. Cut meat into serving pieces; sprinkle with salt and pepper.

2. Combine vegetables, bay leaves, rosemary and thyme in slow cooker. Place beef over vegetables. Pour broth over beef. Cover; cook on LOW 8½ to 9 hours or until beef is fork-tender. Remove beef to serving platter. Arrange vegetables around beef. Remove and discard bay leaves.

3. To make gravy, ladle juices into 2-cup measure; let stand 5 minutes. Skim off and discard fat. Measure remaining juices and heat to a boil in small saucepan. For each cup of juice, mix 2 tablespoons of flour with ¼ cup of cold water until smooth. Stir mixture into boiling juices, stirring constantly 1 minute or until thickened. *Makes 10 to 12 servings*

Best Corned Beef Ever

Cajun Chili

1½ pounds ground beef
2 cans (15 ounces each) Cajun-style mixed vegetables, undrained
2 cans (10¾ ounces each) condensed tomato soup, undiluted
1 can (14½ ounces) diced tomatoes, undrained
3 sausages with Cheddar cheese (about 8 ounces), quartered and sliced into bite-size pieces
Shredded cheddar cheese (optional)

1. Cook and stir ground beef in medium skillet over medium-high heat until no longer pink. Drain well.

2. Place ground beef, mixed vegetables, tomato soup, tomatoes and sausages in slow cooker. Cover; cook on HIGH 2 hours. Serve with shredded cheese, if desired.

Makes 10 servings

Easy Does It

When using ground beef in a slow cooker, brown it first. There are two reasons for taking this extra step. It improves the flavor and color of the final dish, and it also allows you to drain off the fat ahead of time.

Beefy Tostada Pies

2 teaspoons olive oil
1½ cups chopped onion
2 pounds ground beef
1 teaspoon chili powder
1 teaspoon ground cumin
1 teaspoon salt
2 cloves garlic, minced
1 can (15 ounces) tomato sauce
1 cup sliced black olives
8 flour tortillas
4 cups shredded Cheddar cheese
Sour cream, salsa and chopped green onion (optional)

1. Heat oil in large skillet over medium heat. Add onion and cook until tender. Add ground beef, chili powder, cumin, salt and garlic; cook until browned. Stir in tomato sauce; heat through. Stir in black olives.

2. Make foil handles using three 18×2-inch strips of heavy foil. Crisscross foil to form spoke design. Place in slow cooker. Lay one tortilla on foil strips. Spread with meat sauce and layer of cheese. Top with another tortilla, meat sauce and cheese. Repeat layers ending with cheese. Cover and cook on HIGH 1½ hours. To serve, lift out of slow cooker using foil handles and transfer to serving platter. Discard foil. Cut into wedges. Serve with sour cream, salsa and chopped green onion, if desired.

Makes 4 to 5 servings

Cajun Chili

Special Sauerbraten

2 cups dry red wine
2 cups red wine vinegar
2 cups water
2 large onions, sliced
2 large carrots, sliced
¼ cup sugar
1 tablespoon dried parsley flakes
2 teaspoons salt
1 teaspoon mustard seed
4 bay leaves
6 peppercorns
6 whole cloves
4 juniper berries* (optional)
1 beef round tip roast (about 5 pounds)
4 tablespoons all-purpose flour, divided
1 teaspoon salt
¼ teaspoon pepper
2 tablespoons oil
2 tablespoons sugar
⅓ cup gingersnap crumbs

Juniper berries are available in the spice aisle at large supermarkets or from mail order spice purveyors.

1. Stir together wine, vinegar, water, onions, carrots, sugar, parsley, salt, mustard seed, bay leaves, peppercorns, cloves and juniper berries, if desired, in medium saucepan over high heat. Bring to a boil; reduce heat to medium low and simmer 15 minutes. Cool completely. Place roast in large glass bowl or large resealable plastic food storage bag; pour mixture over roast. Cover or seal bag. Marinate in refrigerator up to 2 days, turning once a day.

2. Remove meat from marinade. Strain marinade and discard vegetables, reserving marinade. Dry meat with paper towel. In small bowl, mix 2 tablespoons flour, salt and pepper; use to coat all sides of meat. Heat oil in large skillet over medium heat; add meat and brown on all sides.

3. Place browned meat in slow cooker; add 1½ cups strained marinade. Discard remaining marinade. Cover; cook on LOW 8 hours.

4. Combine sugar, remaining 2 tablespoons flour and gingersnap crumbs; add to slow cooker and stir well. Cover; cook on HIGH 30 minutes.

Makes 6 to 8 servings

Note: Sauerbraten is a German dish that is traditionally marinated 3 or 4 days.

Slow Cooker Meatloaf

1½ pounds ground beef
¾ cup milk
⅔ cup fine dry bread crumbs
2 eggs, beaten
2 tablespoons minced onion
1 teaspoon salt
½ teaspoon ground sage
½ cup ketchup
2 tablespoons brown sugar
1 teaspoon dry mustard

1. Combine beef, milk, bread crumbs, eggs, onion, salt and sage in large bowl. Shape into ball and place in slow cooker. Cover; cook on LOW 5 to 6 hours.

2. Fifteen minutes before serving, combine ketchup, brown sugar and mustard in small bowl. Pour over meatloaf. Cover; cook on HIGH 15 minutes.

Makes 6 servings

Slow Cooker Meatloaf

Broccoli and Beef Pasta

2 cups broccoli florets *or* **1 package
       (10 ounces) frozen broccoli, thawed**
1 onion, thinly sliced
½ teaspoon dried basil leaves
½ teaspoon dried oregano leaves
½ teaspoon dried thyme leaves
**1 can (14½ ounces) Italian-style diced
       tomatoes, undrained**
¾ cup beef broth
1 pound lean ground beef
2 cloves garlic, minced
2 tablespoons tomato paste
2 cups cooked rotini pasta
**3 ounces shredded Cheddar cheese or
       grated Parmesan cheese**

1. Layer broccoli, onion, basil, oregano, thyme, tomatoes with juice and beef broth in slow cooker. Cover; cook on LOW 2½ hours.

2. Combine beef and garlic in large nonstick skillet; cook over high heat 6 to 8 minutes or until meat is no longer pink, breaking meat apart with wooden spoon. Pour off drippings. Add beef mixture to slow cooker. Cover; cook 2 hours.

3. Stir in tomato paste. Add pasta and cheese. Cover; cook 30 minutes or until cheese melts and mixture is heated through. Sprinkle with additional shredded cheese, if desired.

Makes 4 servings

Veal Stew with Horseradish

1¼ pounds lean veal, cut into 1-inch cubes
**2 medium sweet potatoes, peeled and cut
       into 2-inch pieces**
1 can (14½ ounces) diced tomatoes
1 package (10 ounces) frozen corn
1 package (9 ounces) frozen lima beans
1 large onion, chopped
1 cup vegetable broth
1 tablespoon chili powder
1 tablespoon extra-hot horseradish
1 tablespoon honey

1. Place all ingredients in slow cooker. Mix well.

2. Cover; cook on LOW 7 to 8 hours.

Makes 6 servings

Broccoli and Beef Pasta

Veal Stew with Horseradish

Steak San Marino

¼ cup all-purpose flour
1 teaspoon salt
½ teaspoon black pepper
1 beef round steak (about 1½ pounds), cut
    into 4 pieces *or* 2 beef top round
    steaks, cut in half
1 can (8 ounces) tomato sauce
2 carrots, chopped
½ onion, chopped
1 rib celery, chopped
1 teaspoon dried Italian seasoning
½ teaspoon Worcestershire sauce
1 bay leaf
    Hot cooked rice

1. Combine flour, salt and pepper in small bowl. Dredge each steak in flour mixture. Place in slow cooker. Combine tomato sauce, carrots, onion, celery, Italian seasoning, Worcestershire sauce and bay leaf in small bowl; pour into slow cooker. Cover; cook on LOW 8 to 10 hours or on HIGH 4 to 5 hours.

2. Remove and discard bay leaf. Serve steaks and sauce over rice.   *Makes 4 servings*

Easy Does It

Less expensive cuts of beef like flank steak do well in a slow cooker since they have time to become tender and their flavor benefits from the long, low heat.

Spicy Beef and Pepper Fajitas

1 beef flank steak (about 1½ pounds), cut
    into 6 pieces
1 cup chopped onion
2 green bell peppers, cut into ½-inch-wide
    strips
1 jalapeño pepper,* chopped
2 tablespoons chopped fresh cilantro
2 cloves garlic, minced
1 teaspoon chili powder
1 teaspoon ground cumin
½ teaspoon salt
¼ teaspoon ground red pepper
1 can (8 ounces) chopped tomatoes,
    drained
12 (8-inch) flour tortillas
    Toppings, such as sour cream, shredded
        Cheddar cheese and salsa
    Sliced avocado (optional)

*Jalapeño peppers can sting and irritate the skin; wear rubber gloves when handling peppers and do not touch eyes. Wash hands after handling.

1. Combine beef, onion, bell peppers, jalapeño pepper, cilantro, garlic, chili powder, cumin, salt and ground red pepper in slow cooker. Add tomatoes. Cover; cook on LOW 8 to 10 hours.

2. Remove beef from slow cooker and pull into shreds with fork. Return beef to slow cooker. To serve, layer beef mixture on tortillas. Top with toppings; roll up tortillas. Serve with sliced avocado, if desired.   *Makes 12 servings*

Steak San Marino

Beef and Parsnip Stroganoff

1 beef bouillon cube
¾ cup boiling water
1 boneless beef top round steak (about ¾ pound), trimmed
Nonstick olive oil cooking spray
2 cups cubed peeled parsnips or potatoes*
1 medium onion, halved and thinly sliced
¾ pound mushrooms, sliced
2 teaspoons minced garlic
¼ teaspoon black pepper
¼ cup water
1 tablespoon plus 1½ teaspoons all-purpose flour
3 tablespoons reduced-fat sour cream
1½ teaspoons Dijon mustard
¼ teaspoon cornstarch
1 tablespoon chopped fresh parsley
4 ounces wide noodles, cooked and drained

*If using potatoes, cut into 1-inch chunks and do not sauté.

1. Dissolve bouillon cube in ¾ cup boiling water; cool. Meanwhile, cut steak lengthwise in half, then crosswise into ½-inch strips. Spray large nonstick skillet with cooking spray; heat over high heat. Cook and stir beef about 4 minutes or until meat begins to brown. Transfer beef and juices to slow cooker.

2. Spray same skillet with cooking spray; heat over high heat. Add parsnips and onion; cook and stir until browned, about 4 minutes. Add mushrooms, garlic and pepper; cook and stir until mushrooms are tender, about 5 minutes. Transfer mushroom mixture to slow cooker.

3. Stir ¼ cup water into flour in small bowl until smooth. Stir flour mixture into cooled bouillon. Add to slow cooker; stir until blended. Cover;

cook on LOW 4½ to 5 hours or until beef and parsnips are tender.

4. Turn off slow cooker. Remove beef and vegetables with slotted spoon to large bowl; reserve cooking liquid from beef. Blend sour cream, mustard and cornstarch in medium bowl. Gradually add reserved liquid to sour cream mixture; stir well to blend. Stir sour cream mixture into beef mixture. Sprinkle with parsley; serve over noodles. Garnish, if desired.

Makes 4 servings

Glazed Corned Beef

1½ cups water
1 medium onion, sliced
3 strips fresh orange peel
2 whole cloves
3 to 4 pounds corned beef
Additional whole cloves (optional)
Glaze (recipe follows)

1. Combine water, onion, orange peel and cloves in slow cooker. Add corned beef, fat side up. Cover; cook on LOW 7 to 9 hours or until tender.

2. Remove corned beef from slow cooker and score top. Insert additional cloves, if desired.

3. About 30 minutes before serving, place corned beef in ovenproof pan. Preheat oven to 375°F. Prepare Glaze; spoon over corned beef. Bake 20 to 30 minutes, basting occasionally with Glaze.

Makes 8 to 10 servings

Glaze: Combine 2 tablespoons orange juice concentrate, 3 tablespoons honey and 2 teaspoons prepared mustard in small bowl.

Beef and Parsnip Stroganoff

Slow Cooker Pizza Casserole

1½ pounds ground beef, cooked and drained
1 pound sausage, cooked and drained
1 pound corkscrew pasta, cooked and
    drained
4 jars (14 ounces each) pizza sauce
2 cups (8 ounces) shredded mozzarella
    cheese
2 cups freshly grated Parmesan cheese
2 cans (4 ounces each) mushroom stems
    and pieces, drained
2 packages (3 ounces each) sliced
    pepperoni
½ cup finely chopped onion
½ cup finely chopped green pepper
1 clove garlic minced

1. Combine all ingredients in slow cooker.

2. Cover; cook on HIGH 2 hours or LOW
4 hours.   *Makes 6 servings*

Beef Bourguignon

1 to 2 boneless beef top sirloin steaks
    (about 3 pounds)
½ cup all-purpose flour
4 slices bacon, diced
2 medium carrots, diced
8 small new red potatoes, unpeeled, cut
    into quarters
8 to 10 mushrooms, sliced
20 to 24 pearl onions
3 cloves garlic, minced
1 bay leaf
1 teaspoon dried marjoram leaves
½ teaspoon dried thyme leaves
½ teaspoon salt
    Black pepper to taste
2½ cups Burgundy wine or beef broth

1. Cut beef into ½-inch pieces. Coat beef with
flour, shaking off excess. Set aside.

2. Cook bacon in large skillet over medium heat
until partially cooked. Add beef; cook until
browned. Remove beef and bacon with slotted
spoon.

3. Layer carrots, potatoes, mushrooms, onions,
garlic, bay leaf, marjoram, thyme, salt, pepper,
beef and bacon mixture in slow cooker. Pour
wine over all. Cover; cook on LOW 8 to 9 hours
or until beef is tender. Remove and discard bay
leaf.   *Makes 10 to 12 servings*

Slow Cooker Pizza Casserole

Beef Bourguignon

Poultry or Pork in a Pot

Think there's nothing new to do with chicken or pork? Turn to your slow cooker. Whether it's Mile-High Enchilada Pie or Easy Chicken Alfredo, these recipes offer delectable new ways to escape the humdrum.

Spicy Asian Pork Filling

1 boneless pork sirloin roast (about 3 pounds)
½ cup tamari or soy sauce
1 tablespoon chili garlic sauce or chili paste
2 teaspoons minced fresh ginger
2 tablespoons water
1 tablespoon cornstarch
2 teaspoons dark sesame oil

1. Cut roast into 2- to 3-inch chunks. Combine pork, tamari sauce, chili garlic sauce and ginger in slow cooker; mix well. Cover; cook on LOW 8 to 10 hours or until pork is fork tender.

2. Remove roast from cooking liquid; cool slightly. Trim and discard excess fat. Shred pork using 2 forks.

3. Let liquid stand 5 minutes to allow fat to rise. Skim off fat.

4. Blend water, cornstarch and sesame oil; whisk into liquid. Cook on HIGH until thickened. Add shredded meat to slow cooker; mix well. Cook 15 to 30 minutes or until hot.

Makes 5½ cups filling

Spicy Asian Pork Bundles: Place ¼ cup pork filling into large lettuce leaves. Wrap to enclose. Makes about 20 bundles.

Moo Shu Pork: Lightly spread plum sauce over warm small flour tortillas. Spoon ¼ cup pork filling and ¼ cup stir-fried vegetables into flour tortillas. Wrap to enclose. Makes enough to fill about 20 tortillas.

Spicy Asian Pork Filling

Chicken Curry

 2 boneless skinless chicken breast halves,
    cut into ¾-inch pieces
 1 small onion, sliced
 1 cup coarsely chopped apple, divided
 3 tablespoons raisins
 1 clove garlic, minced
 1 teaspoon curry powder
 ¼ teaspoon ground ginger
 ⅓ cup water
 1½ teaspoons chicken bouillon granules
 1½ teaspoons all-purpose flour
 ¼ cup sour cream
 ½ teaspoon cornstarch
 ½ cup uncooked white rice

1. Combine chicken, onion, ¾ cup apple, raisins, garlic, curry powder and ginger in slow cooker. Combine water and bouillon granules in small bowl until dissolved. Stir in flour until smooth. Add to slow cooker. Cover; cook on LOW 3½ to 4 hours or until onions are tender and chicken is no longer pink.

2. Combine sour cream and cornstarch in large bowl. Turn off slow cooker. Transfer all cooking liquid from chicken mixture to sour cream mixture; stir until combined. Stir mixture back into slow cooker. Cover and let stand 5 to 10 minutes or until sauce is heated through.

3. Meanwhile, cook rice according to package directions. Serve chicken curry over rice; garnish with remaining ¼ cup apple.   *Makes 2 servings*

Hint: For a special touch, sprinkle chicken with green onion slivers just before serving.

Sweet 'n' Spicy Ribs

 5 cups prepared barbecue sauce*
 ¾ cup brown sugar
 ¼ cup honey
 2 tablespoons Cajun seasoning
 1 tablespoon garlic powder
 1 tablespoon onion powder
 6 pounds pork or beef back ribs, cut into
    3-rib portions

Barbecue sauce adds a significant flavor to this recipe. Use your favorite sauce to ensure you fully enjoy the dish.

1. In medium bowl, stir together barbecue sauce, brown sugar, honey, Cajun seasoning, garlic powder and onion powder. Remove and reserve 1-cup of mixture and refrigerate.

2. Place ribs in slow cooker and cover with barbecue mixture. Cover; cook on LOW 8 hours or until meat is very tender.

3. Uncover and skim fat from surface. Use reserved sauce for dipping or to coat top of ribs.
Makes 10 servings

Easy Does It

For even tastier ribs, brown them before slow cooking. Preheat a broiler and arrange ribs on the broiling pan. Broil 6 inches from the heat for about 5 minutes a side until lightly browned.

Sweet 'n' Spicy Ribs

San Marino Chicken

1 chicken (3 pounds), skinned and cut up
¼ cup all-purpose flour
1 can (8 ounces) tomato sauce
⅓ cup chopped sun-dried tomatoes packed in oil
¼ cup red wine
1 tablespoon grated lemon peel
2 cups sliced mushrooms
2 cups *French's*® French Fried Onions, divided
Hot cooked rice or pasta (optional)

1. Lightly coat chicken pieces with flour. Place chicken in slow cooker. Add tomato sauce, sun-dried tomatoes, wine and lemon peel. Cover and cook on LOW setting for 4 hours (or on HIGH for 2 hours).

2. Add mushrooms and *1 cup* French Fried Onions. Cover and cook on LOW setting for 2 hours (or on HIGH for 1 hour) until chicken is no longer pink near bone. Remove chicken to heated platter. Skim fat from sauce.

3. Serve chicken with hot cooked rice or pasta, if desired. Spoon sauce on top and sprinkle with remaining onions.   *Makes 4 servings*

Greek-Style Chicken

6 boneless skinless chicken thighs
½ teaspoon salt
½ teaspoon black pepper
1 tablespoon olive oil
½ cup chicken broth
1 lemon, thinly sliced
¼ cup pitted kalamata olives
½ teaspoon dried oregano leaves
1 clove garlic, minced
Hot cooked orzo or rice

1. Remove visible fat from chicken; sprinkle chicken with salt and pepper. Heat oil in large skillet over medium-high heat. Brown chicken on all sides. Place chicken in slow cooker.

2. Add broth, lemon, olives, oregano and garlic to slow cooker. Cover; cook on LOW 5 to 6 hours or until chicken is tender. Serve with orzo.   *Makes 4 to 6 servings*

San Marino Chicken

Greek-Style Chicken

Simple Coq au Vin

    4 chicken legs
      Salt and black pepper
    2 tablespoons olive oil
    ½ pound mushrooms, sliced
    1 onion, sliced into rings
    ½ cup red wine
    ½ teaspoon dried basil leaves
    ½ teaspoon dried thyme leaves
    ½ teaspoon dried oregano leaves
      Hot cooked rice

1. Sprinkle chicken with salt and pepper. Heat oil in large skillet; brown chicken on both sides. Remove chicken and place in slow cooker. Sauté mushrooms and onion in same skillet. Add wine; stir and scrape brown bits from bottom of skillet.

2. Add mixture to slow cooker. Sprinkle with basil, thyme and oregano. Cover; cook on LOW 8 to 10 hours or on HIGH 3 to 4 hours. Serve chicken and sauce over rice.   *Makes 4 servings*

Easy Does It

The slow cooker is the easy way to braise which means to cook food tightly covered for a long time over low heat. Classic braises, like coq au vin, are virtually foolproof in a slow cooker.

Meatball Grinders

    1 can (15 ounces) diced tomatoes, drained
      and juices reserved
    1 can (8 ounces) reduced-sodium tomato
      sauce
    ¼ cup chopped onion
    2 tablespoons tomato paste
    1 teaspoon dried Italian seasoning
    1 pound ground chicken
    ½ cup fresh whole wheat or white bread
      crumbs (1 slice bread)
    1 egg white, lightly beaten
    3 tablespoons finely chopped fresh parsley
    2 cloves garlic, minced
    ¼ teaspoon salt
    ⅛ teaspoon black pepper
    4 small hard rolls, split
    2 tablespoons grated Parmesan cheese

1. Combine diced tomatoes, ½ cup reserved juice, tomato sauce, onion, tomato paste and Italian seasoning in slow cooker. Cover; cook on LOW 3 to 4 hours or until onions are soft.

2. During the last 30 minutes of cooking time, prepare meatballs. Combine chicken, bread crumbs, egg white, parsley, garlic, salt and pepper in medium bowl. With wet hands form mixture into 12 to 16 meatballs. Spray medium nonstick skillet with cooking spray; heat over medium heat until hot. Add meatballs; cook about 8 to 10 minutes or until well browned on all sides. Remove meatballs to slow cooker; cook 1 to 2 hours or until meatballs are no longer pink in centers and are heated through.

3. Place 3 to 4 meatballs in each roll. Spoon sauce over meatballs. Sprinkle with cheese.
    Makes 4 servings

Simple Coq au Vin

Chicken Fajitas with Cowpoke Barbecue Sauce

Cowpoke Barbecue Sauce
  1 can (8 ounces) tomato sauce
  ⅓ cup chopped green onions
  ¼ cup ketchup
  2 tablespoons water
  2 tablespoons orange juice
  1 tablespoon cider vinegar
  1 tablespoon chili sauce
  2 cloves garlic, finely chopped
  ½ teaspoon vegetable oil
    Dash Worcestershire sauce

Fajitas
  10 ounces boneless skinless chicken
      breasts, cut into ½-inch strips
  2 green or red bell peppers, thinly sliced
  1 cup sliced onion
  2 cups tomato wedges
  4 (6-inch) warm flour tortillas

1. Combine all Cowpoke Barbecue Sauce ingredients in slow cooker. Cover; cook on HIGH 1½ hours.

2. Spray large nonstick skillet with nonstick cooking spray. Add chicken and cook over medium heat until browned. Reduce slow cooker heat to LOW. Add cooked chicken, bell peppers and onion to slow cooker. Stir until well coated. Cover; cook 3 to 4 hours or until chicken is no longer pink and vegetables are tender.

3. Add tomatoes; cover and cook 30 to 45 minutes or until heated through. Serve with warm tortillas. *Makes 4 servings*

Chicken Pilaf

  2 pounds chopped cooked chicken
  2 cans (8 ounces each) tomato sauce
  2½ cups water
  1⅓ cups uncooked rice
  1 cup chopped green bell pepper
  1 cup chopped onion
  1 cup chopped celery
  ⅔ cup sliced black olives
  ¼ cup sliced almonds
  ¼ cup (½ stick) margarine or butter
  2 cloves garlic, minced
  2½ teaspoons salt
  ½ teaspoon ground allspice
  ½ teaspoon ground turmeric
  ¼ teaspoon curry powder
  ¼ teaspoon black pepper

1. Combine all ingredients in slow cooker; stir well.

2. Cover; cook on LOW 6 to 9 hours or on HIGH 3 hours. *Makes 10 servings*

Easy Does It

For recipes calling for cooked chicken, purchase a rotisserie or other pre-cooked chicken in the supermarket deli. You can often purchase pre-cut vegetables from the produce department, too.

Chicken Pilaf

Glazed Pork Loin

1 bag (1 pound) baby carrots
4 boneless pork loin chops
1 jar (8 ounces) apricot preserves

1. Place carrots in bottom of slow cooker. Place pork on carrots and brush with preserves.

2. Cover; cook on HIGH 4 hours or on LOW 8 hours. *Makes 4 servings*

Serving Suggestion: Serve with seasoned or cheese-flavored instant mashed potatoes.

Mexicali Chicken

2 medium green bell peppers, cut into thin strips
1 large onion, quartered and thinly sliced
4 chicken thighs
4 chicken drumsticks
1 tablespoon chili powder
2 teaspoons dried oregano leaves
1 jar (16 ounces) chipotle salsa
½ cup ketchup
2 teaspoons ground cumin
½ teaspoon salt
Hot cooked noodles

1. Place bell peppers and onion in slow cooker; top with chicken. Sprinkle chili powder and oregano evenly over chicken. Add salsa. Cover; cook on LOW 7 to 8 hours or until chicken is tender.

2. Remove chicken pieces to serving bowl; keep warm. Stir ketchup, cumin and salt into liquid in slow cooker. Cook, uncovered, on HIGH 15 minutes or until hot.

3. Pour mixture over chicken. Serve with noodles. *Makes 4 servings*

Tip: For thicker sauce, blend 1 tablespoon cornstarch and 2 tablespoons water. Stir into cooking liquid with ketchup, cumin and salt.

Glazed Pork Loin

Mexicali Chicken

Pork Roast Landaise

2 tablespoons olive oil
2½ pounds boneless center cut pork loin
    roast
    Salt and pepper
1 medium sweet onion, diced
2 large cloves garlic, minced
2 teaspoons dried thyme
2 cups chicken stock, divided
2 tablespoons cornstarch or arrowroot
¼ cup red wine vinegar
¼ cup sugar
½ cup port or sherry wine
2 parsnips, cut into ¾-inch slices
1½ cups pitted prunes
3 pears, cored and sliced ¾-inch thick

1. Heat olive oil in large saucepan over medium-high heat. Season pork roast with salt and pepper and brown on all sides. Place browned roast in slow cooker.

2. Add onion and garlic to saucepan. Cook and stir over medium heat 2 to 3 minutes. Stir in thyme. Add onion mixture to slow cooker.

3. In small bowl, mix ¼ cup of chicken stock with the cornstarch; set aside.

4. Combine vinegar and sugar in same saucepan in which onion and garlic were cooked. Cook over medium heat, stirring constantly, until mixture thickens into syrup. Add port and cook 1 minute more. Add remaining 1¾ cups chicken stock. Whisk in cornstarch and cook until smooth and slightly thickened. Pour into slow cooker.

5. Cover; cook on HIGH 4 hours or on LOW 8 hours. During the last 30 minutes of cooking, add parsnips, prunes and pears. Serve over rice or mashed potatoes or with French bread to dunk in the gravy. *Makes 4 to 6 servings*

Campbell's® Lemon Chicken

2 cans (10¾ ounces each) CAMPBELL'S®
    Condensed Cream of Chicken Soup *or*
    98% Fat Free Cream of Chicken Soup
½ cup water
¼ cup lemon juice
2 teaspoons Dijon-style mustard
1½ teaspoons garlic powder
8 large carrots, thickly sliced (about
    6 cups)
8 skinless, boneless chicken breast halves
    (about 2 pounds)
8 cups hot cooked egg noodles
    Grated Parmesan cheese

1. In slow cooker mix soup, water, lemon juice, mustard, garlic powder and carrots. Add chicken and turn to coat. Cover and cook on **low** 7 to 8 hours or until chicken is done.

2. Serve over noodles. Sprinkle with cheese.
Makes 8 servings

*Bottom to top: Campbell's® Lemon Chicken,
Campbell's® Asian Tomato Beef (page 116)*

Simple Shredded Pork Tacos

2 pounds boneless pork roast
1 cup salsa
1 can (4 ounces) chopped green chilies
½ teaspoon garlic salt
½ teaspoon pepper

1. Place all ingredients in slow cooker.

2. Cover; cook on LOW 8 to 10 hours, or until meat is tender. To serve, use 2 forks to shred pork. *Makes 6 servings*

Serving Suggestion: Serve with tortillas and your favorite condiments.

Chicken in Honey Sauce

4 to 6 boneless skinless chicken breasts
Salt
Black pepper
2 cups honey
1 cup soy sauce
½ cup ketchup
¼ cup oil
2 cloves garlic, minced
Sesame seeds

1. Place chicken in slow cooker; season with salt and pepper.

2. Combine honey, soy sauce, ketchup, oil and garlic in medium bowl. Pour over chicken in slow cooker. Cover; cook on LOW 6 to 8 hours or on HIGH 3 to 4 hours.

3. Garnish with sesame seeds before serving.
Makes 4 to 6 servings

Italian Chicken with Sausage and Peppers

2½ pounds chicken pieces
2 tablespoons olive oil
½ to ¾ pounds Italian sweet sausage
2 green bell peppers, chopped
1 onion, chopped
1 carrot, finely chopped
2 cloves garlic, minced
1 can (15 ounces) tomato sauce
1 can (19 ounces) tomato soup
¼ teaspoon dried oregano
¼ teaspoon basil
1 bay leaf
Salt and pepper

1. Rinse chicken; pat dry. Heat oil in large skillet over medium-high heat. Add chicken skin side down. Cook about 10 minutes, turning to brown both sides. Remove and reserve.

2. Add sausage to skillet and cook 4 to 5 minutes or until browned. Remove, cut into 1-inch pieces and reserve. Drain off all but 1 tablespoon fat from skillet.

3. Add bell peppers, onion, carrot and garlic to skillet. Cook 4 to 5 minutes or until vegetables are tender.

4. Add tomato sauce, tomato soup, oregano, basil and bay leaf; stir well. Season with salt and pepper. Transfer to slow cooker.

5. Add chicken and sausage to slow cooker. Cover; cook on LOW 6 to 8 hours or on HIGH 4 to 6 hours. *Makes 6 servings*

Italian Chicken with Sausage and Peppers

Harvest Drums

**1 package (about 1¼ pounds) PERDUE®
Fresh Skinless Chicken Drumsticks**
½ teaspoon dried Italian herb seasoning
Salt and ground pepper
3 bacon slices, diced
2 cans (14½ ounces each) pasta-ready
tomatoes with cheeses
1 small onion, chopped
¼ cup red wine
1 clove garlic, minced
1 small zucchini, scrubbed and julienned
1 package (12 ounces) angel hair pasta,
cooked and drained

Sprinkle chicken with Italian seasoning and salt
and pepper to taste. In large, nonstick skillet
over medium-low heat, cook bacon about
5 minutes, until crisp. Remove from skillet; drain
and crumble. Increase heat to medium-high. Add
chicken to bacon drippings (or replace drippings
with 1½ tablespoons olive oil); cook 4 to
5 minutes on all sides or until brown, turning
often.

In large slow cooker, combine tomatoes, bacon,
onion, wine and garlic. Add chicken; cook on
HIGH 1½ to 1¾ hours, or until fork-tender. Add
zucchini during last 5 minutes of cooking. Serve
chicken and vegetables over angel hair pasta.

Makes 3 to 4 servings

Easy Chicken Alfredo

**1½ pounds chicken breast, cut into ½-inch
pieces**
1 medium onion, chopped
1 tablespoon extra-virgin olive oil
1 tablespoon dried chives
1 tablespoon dried basil leaves
1 teaspoon lemon pepper
¼ teaspoon ground ginger
½ pound broccoli, coarsely chopped
1 red bell pepper, chopped
1 can (8 ounces) sliced water chestnuts,
drained
1 cup baby carrots
3 cloves garlic, minced
1 jar (16 ounces) Alfredo sauce
1 package (8 ounces) wide egg noodles,
cooked and drained

1. Combine chicken, onion, olive oil, chives, basil,
lemon pepper and ginger in slow cooker; stir
thoroughly. Add broccoli, bell pepper, water
chestnuts, carrots and garlic. Mix well.

2. Cover; cook on LOW 8 hours or on HIGH
3 hours.

3. Add Alfredo sauce and cook an additional
30 minutes or until heated through.

4. Serve over hot egg noodles.

Makes 6 servings

Easy Chicken Alfredo

Harvest Ham Supper

6 carrots, sliced in half lengthwise
3 sweet potatoes, sliced in half lengthwise
1½ pounds boneless ham
1 cup maple syrup

1. Place carrots and potatoes in bottom of slow cooker to form a rack. Place ham on top of vegetables. Pour syrup over ham and vegetables.

2. Cover; cook on LOW 6 to 8 hours.

Makes 6 servings

Harvest Ham Supper

South-of-the-Border Cumin Chicken

1 package (16 ounces) frozen bell pepper
    stir-fry mixture or 3 bell peppers,
    sliced thin*
4 chicken drumsticks
4 chicken thighs
1 can (14½ ounces) stewed tomatoes
2 teaspoons sugar
1 teaspoon dried oregano leaves
1¾ teaspoons ground cumin, divided
1¼ teaspoons salt
1 tablespoon mild pepper sauce
¼ cup chopped fresh cilantro leaves
1 to 2 medium limes, cut in wedges

*If using fresh bell peppers, add 1 small onion, chopped.

1. Place bell pepper mixture in slow cooker; place chicken on top.

2. Combine stewed tomatoes, sugar, oregano, 1 teaspoon of cumin, salt and pepper sauce in large bowl. Pour over chicken-bell pepper mixture. Cover; cook on HIGH 4 hours or on LOW 8 hours or until meat is just beginning to fall off bone.

3. Place chicken in shallow serving bowl. Stir remaining ¾ teaspoon cumin into tomato mixture and pour over chicken. Sprinkle with cilantro and serve with lime wedges. Serve over cooked rice or with toasted corn tortillas.

Makes 4 servings

South-of-the-Border Cumin Chicken

Chicken Stew with Dumplings

- 2 cans (about 14 ounces each) chicken broth, divided
- 2 cups sliced carrots
- 1 cup chopped onion
- 1 large green bell pepper, sliced
- ½ cup sliced celery
- ⅔ cup all-purpose flour
- 1 pound boneless skinless chicken breasts, cut into 1-inch pieces
- 1 large potato, unpeeled and cut into 1-inch pieces
- 6 ounces mushrooms, cut in half
- ¾ cup frozen peas
- 1 teaspoon dried basil leaves
- ¾ teaspoon dried rosemary leaves
- ¼ teaspoon dried tarragon leaves
- ¾ to 1 teaspoon salt
- ¼ teaspoon black pepper
- ¼ cup heavy cream

Herb Dumplings
- 1 cup biscuit baking mix
- ¼ teaspoon dried basil leaves
- ¼ teaspoon dried rosemary leaves
- ⅛ teaspoon dried tarragon leaves
- ⅓ cup reduced-fat (2%) milk

1. Reserve 1 cup chicken broth. Combine carrots, onion, green bell pepper, celery and remaining chicken broth in slow cooker. Cover; cook on LOW 2 hours.

2. Stir flour into reserved 1 cup broth until smooth. Stir into slow cooker. Add chicken, potato, mushrooms, peas, 1 teaspoon basil, ¾ teaspoon rosemary and ¼ teaspoon tarragon to slow cooker. Cover; cook 4 hours or until vegetables are tender and chicken is no longer pink in center. Stir in salt, black pepper and heavy cream.

3. Combine baking mix, ¼ teaspoon basil, ¼ teaspoon rosemary and ¼ teaspoon tarragon in small bowl. Stir in milk to form soft dough. Spoon dumpling mixture on top of stew in 4 large spoonfuls. Cook, uncovered, 30 minutes. Cover; cook 30 to 45 minutes or until dumplings are firm and toothpick inserted in center comes out clean. Serve in shallow bowls.

Makes 4 servings

Campbell's® Creamy Chicken & Wild Rice

- 2 cans (10¾ ounces each) CAMPBELL'S® Condensed Cream of Chicken Soup *or* 98% Fat Free Cream of Chicken Soup
- 1½ cups water
- 1 package (6 ounces) seasoned long grain and wild rice mix
- 4 large carrots, thickly sliced (about 3 cups)
- 8 skinless, boneless chicken breast halves (about 2 pounds)

In slow cooker mix soup, water, rice and carrots. Add chicken and turn to coat. Cover and cook on *low* 7 to 8 hours or until chicken and rice are done.

Makes 8 servings

Chicken Stew with Dumplings

Ale'd Pork and Sauerkraut

1 jar (32 ounces) sauerkraut, undrained
1½ tablespoons sugar
1 can (12 ounces) dark beer or ale
3½ pounds pork shoulder or pork butt
½ teaspoon salt
¼ teaspoon garlic powder
¼ teaspoon black pepper
Paprika

1. Pour sauerkraut into slow cooker. Sprinkle sugar evenly over sauerkraut, and pour beer over all. Place pork, fat side up, on top of sauerkraut mixture; sprinkle evenly with remaining ingredients. Cover; cook on HIGH 6 hours.

2. Place pork on serving platter and, using a slotted spoon, remove sauerkraut and arrange around pork. Spoon about ½ to ¾ cup cooking liquid over sauerkraut, if desired.

Makes 6 to 8 servings

Easy Does It

Sauerkraut is chopped cabbage that has been salted and fermented. It is available in jars or cans. You can also purchase fresh sauerkraut in plastic bags in the produce section of many supermarkets.

Forty-Clove Chicken

1 frying chicken (3 pounds), cut into serving pieces
Salt and black pepper
1 to 2 tablespoons olive oil
¼ cup dry white wine
⅛ cup dry vermouth
2 tablespoons chopped fresh parsley *or* 2 teaspoons dried parsley leaves
2 teaspoons dried basil leaves
1 teaspoon dried oregano leaves
Pinch of red pepper flakes
40 cloves garlic (about 2 heads*), peeled
4 ribs celery, sliced
Juice and peel of 1 lemon
Fresh herbs (optional)

*The whole garlic bulb is called a head.

1. Remove skin from chicken, if desired. Sprinkle chicken with salt and pepper. Heat oil in large skillet over medium heat. Add chicken; cook 10 minutes or until browned on all sides. Remove to platter.

2. Combine wine, vermouth, parsley, basil, oregano and red pepper flakes in large bowl. Add garlic and celery; coat well. Transfer garlic and celery to slow cooker with slotted spoon. Add chicken to remaining wine and herb mixture; coat well. Place chicken on top of celery in slow cooker. Sprinkle lemon juice and peel in slow cooker; add any remaining wine and herb mixture. Cover; cook on LOW 6 hours or until chicken is no longer pink in center. Garnish with fresh herbs, if desired.

Makes 4 to 6 servings

Ale'd Pork and Sauerkraut

Mile-High Enchilada Pie

8 (6-inch) corn tortillas
1 jar (12 ounces) prepared salsa
1 can (15½ ounces) kidney beans, rinsed
   and drained
1 cup shredded cooked chicken
1 cup shredded Monterey Jack cheese
   with jalapeño peppers

Prepare foil handles for slow cooker (see tip); place in slow cooker. Place 1 tortilla on bottom of slow cooker. Top with small amount of salsa, beans, chicken and cheese. Continue layering using remaining ingredients, ending with cheese. Cover; cook on LOW 6 to 8 hours or on HIGH 3 to 4 hours. Pull out by foil handles.

Makes 4 to 6 servings

Mile-High Enchilada Pie

Easy Does It

To make lifting food out of a slow cooker easy, create foil handles. Crisscross three 18×2-inch strips of heavy duty foil in a spoke design. Place in the slow cooker and position food on top.

3-Cheese Chicken & Noodles

3 cups chopped cooked chicken
1½ cups cottage cheese
1 can (10¾ ounces) condensed cream of
   chicken soup, undiluted
1 package (8 ounces) wide egg noodles,
   cooked and drained
1 cup grated Monterey Jack cheese
½ cup diced celery
½ cup diced onion
½ cup diced green bell pepper
½ cup diced red bell pepper
½ cup grated Parmesan cheese
½ cup chicken broth
1 can (4 ounces) sliced mushrooms,
   drained
2 tablespoons butter, melted
½ teaspoon dried thyme leaves

Combine all ingredients in slow cooker. Stir to coat evenly. Cover; cook on LOW 6 to 10 hours or on HIGH 3 to 4 hours. *Makes 6 servings*

3-Cheese Chicken & Noodles

Campbell's® Golden Mushroom Pork & Apples

2 cans (10¾ ounces each) CAMPBELL'S®
   Condensed Golden Mushroom Soup
½ cup water
1 tablespoon brown sugar
1 tablespoon Worcestershire sauce
1 teaspoon dried thyme leaves, crushed
4 large Granny Smith apples, sliced (about
   4 cups)
2 large onions, sliced (about 2 cups)
8 boneless pork chops, ¾ inch thick (about
   2 pounds)

In slow cooker mix soup, water, brown sugar, Worcestershire and thyme. Add apples, onions and pork. Cover and cook on **low** 8 to 9 hours or until pork is tender.   *Makes 8 servings*

Lemony Roasted Chicken

1 fryer or roasting chicken (3 to 4 pounds)
½ cup chopped onion
2 tablespoons butter
   Juice of one lemon
1 tablespoon chopped fresh parsley
2 teaspoons grated lemon peel
¼ teaspoon salt
¼ teaspoon dried thyme leaves

Rinse chicken and pat dry with paper towels. Remove and discard any excess fat. Place onion in chicken cavity and rub skin with butter. Place chicken in slow cooker. Squeeze juice of lemon over chicken. Sprinkle with grated lemon peel, salt and thyme. Cover; cook on LOW 6 to 8 hours.   *Makes 6 servings*

Country Captain Chicken

4 boneless skinless chicken thighs
2 tablespoons all-purpose flour
2 tablespoons vegetable oil, divided
1 cup chopped green bell pepper
1 large onion, chopped
1 rib celery, chopped
1 clove garlic, minced
¼ cup chicken broth
2 cups canned crushed tomatoes or diced
   fresh tomatoes
½ cup golden raisins
1½ teaspoons curry powder
1 teaspoon salt
¼ teaspoon paprika
¼ teaspoon black pepper
2 cups hot cooked rice

1. Coat chicken with flour; set aside. Heat 1 tablespoon oil in large skillet over medium-high heat until hot. Add bell pepper, onion, celery and garlic. Cook and stir 5 minutes or until vegetables are tender. Place vegetables in slow cooker.

2. Heat remaining 1 tablespoon oil in same skillet over medium-high heat. Add chicken; cook 5 minutes per side until browned. Place chicken in slow cooker.

3. Pour broth into skillet. Heat over medium-high heat, stirring frequently and scraping up any browned bits from bottom of skillet. Pour liquid into slow cooker. Add tomatoes, raisins, curry powder, salt, paprika and black pepper. Cover; cook on LOW 3 hours. Serve chicken with sauce over rice.   *Makes 4 servings*

Bottom to top: Campbell's® Golden Mushroom Pork & Apples,
Campbell's® Savory Pot Roast (page 108)

Hearty Cassoulet

1 tablespoon olive oil
1 large onion, finely chopped
4 boneless skinless chicken thighs (about
    1 pound), chopped
¼ pound smoked turkey sausage, finely
    chopped
3 cloves garlic, minced
1 teaspoon dried thyme leaves
½ teaspoon black pepper
4 tablespoons tomato paste
2 tablespoons water
3 cans (about 15 ounces each) Great
    Northern beans, rinsed and drained
½ cup dry bread crumbs
3 tablespoons minced fresh parsley

1. Heat oil in large skillet over medium heat until hot. Add onion, cook and stir 5 minutes or until onion is tender. Stir in chicken, sausage, garlic, thyme and pepper. Cook 5 minutes or until chicken and sausage are browned.

2. Remove skillet from heat; stir in tomato paste and water until blended. Place beans and chicken mixture in slow cooker. Cover; cook on LOW 4 to 4½ hours. Just before serving, combine bread crumbs and parsley in small bowl. Sprinkle over top of cassoulet.

Makes 6 servings

Pineapple Chicken and Sweet Potatoes

⅔ cup plus 3 tablespoons all-purpose flour,
    divided
1 teaspoon salt
1 teaspoon ground nutmeg
½ teaspoon ground cinnamon
⅛ teaspoon onion powder
⅛ teaspoon black pepper
6 chicken breasts
3 sweet potatoes, peeled and sliced
1 can (10¾ ounces) condensed cream of
    chicken soup, undiluted
½ cup pineapple juice
¼ pound mushrooms, sliced
2 teaspoons packed light brown sugar
½ teaspoon grated orange peel
    Hot cooked rice

1. Combine ⅔ cup flour, salt, nutmeg, cinnamon, onion powder and black pepper in large bowl. Thoroughly coat chicken in flour mixture. Place sweet potatoes on bottom of slow cooker. Top with chicken.

2. Combine soup, pineapple juice, mushrooms, remaining 3 tablespoons flour, brown sugar and orange peel in medium bowl; stir well. Pour soup mixture into slow cooker. Cover; cook on LOW 8 to 10 hours or on HIGH 3 to 4 hours. Serve chicken and sauce over rice.

Make 6 servings

Pineapple Chicken and Sweet Potatoes

Moroccan Chicken Tagine

**3 pounds chicken, cut into serving pieces
  and skin removed**
2 cups chicken broth
**1 can (14½ ounces) diced tomatoes,
  undrained**
2 onions, chopped
1 cup dried apricots, chopped
4 cloves garlic, minced
2 teaspoons ground cumin
1 teaspoon ground cinnamon
1 teaspoon ground ginger
½ teaspoon ground coriander
½ teaspoon ground red pepper
6 sprigs fresh cilantro
1 tablespoon cornstarch
1 tablespoon water
**1 can (15 ounces) chick-peas (garbanzo
  beans), drained and rinsed**
2 tablespoons chopped fresh cilantro
¼ cup slivered almonds, toasted
  Hot cooked couscous or rice

1. Place chicken in slow cooker. Combine broth, tomatoes with juice, onions, apricots, garlic, cumin, cinnamon, ginger, coriander, red pepper and cilantro sprigs in medium bowl; pour over chicken. Cover; cook on LOW 4 to 5 hours or until chicken is no longer pink in center. Transfer chicken to serving platter; cover to keep warm.

2. Combine cornstarch and water in small bowl; mix until smooth. Stir cornstarch mixture and chick-peas into slow cooker. Cover; cook on HIGH 15 minutes or until sauce is thickened. Pour sauce over chicken. Sprinkle with almonds and cilantro. Serve with couscous.

Makes 4 to 6 servings

Tip: To toast almonds, heat small nonstick skillet over medium-high heat. Add almonds; cook and stir about 3 minutes or until golden brown. Remove from pan at once. Let cool before adding to other ingredients.

Sweet Kraut Chops

3 pounds pork chops
½ teaspoon garlic powder
½ teaspoon pepper
1 bag (32 ounces) sauerkraut
1 cup applesauce

1. Place pork chops in slow cooker. Sprinkle with garlic powder and pepper. Pour sauerkraut and then applesauce over pork.

2. Cover; cook on LOW 6 to 8 hours.

Makes 6 to 8 servings

Moroccan Chicken Tagine

Sweet Kraut Chops

Sweet 'n' Slow

The slow cooker's moist,

even heat makes perfect

puddings and custards.

Fruit sauces and desserts

are sweet simplicity, too.

You can even turn out

Chunky Sweet Spiced

Apple Butter without

turning on the stove.

Cherry Flan

5 eggs
½ cup sugar
½ teaspoon salt
¾ cup flour
1 can (12 ounces) evaporated milk
1 teaspoon vanilla
1 bag (16 ounces) frozen, pitted dark
    sweet cherries, thawed
    Sweetened whipped cream or cherry
    vanilla ice cream (optional)

1. Grease inside of slow cooker.

2. Beat eggs, sugar and salt in large bowl of electric mixer at high speed until thick. Add flour; stir until smooth. Stir in evaporated milk and vanilla.

3. Pour batter into prepared slow cooker. Place cherries evenly over batter. Cover; cook on LOW 3½ to 4 hours or until flan is set. Serve warm with whipped cream or ice cream, if desired.

Makes 6 servings

Note: A yummy dessert that is like a custard and a cake mixed together. It is best served warm and is especially delicious when topped with whipped cream or ice cream.

Cherry Flan

Pineapple Daiquiri Sundae

1 pineapple, cored, peeled, and cut into
    ½-inch chunks
½ cup dark rum
½ cup sugar
3 tablespoons lime juice
    Peel of 2 limes, cut in long strands
1 tablespoon cornstarch or arrowroot

1. Place all ingredients in slow cooker; mix well. Cover; cook on HIGH 3 to 4 hours. Serve hot over ice cream, pound cake or shortcakes. Garnish with a few fresh raspberries and mint leaves, if desired.   *Makes 4 to 6 servings*

Variation: Substitute 1 can (20 ounces) crushed pineapple, drained, for the fresh pineapple. Cook on HIGH 3 hours.

Easy Does It

There are special baking pans available that are made to fit inside a slow cooker, but regular baking pans, casserole and soufflé dishes work, too. Just make sure there is some space between the baking dish and the side of the slow cooker.

Peach-Pecan Upside-Down Cake

1 can (8½ ounces) peach slices
⅓ cup packed brown sugar
2 tablespoons butter or margarine, melted
¼ cup chopped pecans
1 package (16 ounces) pound cake mix
½ teaspoon almond extract
    Whipped cream (optional)

1. Generously grease 7½-inch slow cooker bread-and-cake bake pan or casserole dish; set aside.

2. Drain peach slices, reserving 1 tablespoon of juice. Combine reserved peach juice, brown sugar and butter in prepared bake pan. Arrange peach slices on top of brown sugar mixture. Sprinkle with pecans.

3. Prepare cake mix according to package directions; stir in almond extract. Spread over peach mixture. Cover pan. Make foil handles as described below for easier removal of pan from slow cooker. Place pan into slow cooker. Cover; cook on HIGH 3 hours.

4. Use foil handles to remove pan from slow cooker. Cool, uncovered, on wire rack for 10 minutes. Run narrow spatula around sides of pan; invert onto serving plate. Serve warm with whipped cream, if desired.   *Makes 10 servings*

Foil Handles: Tear off three 18×2-inch strips of heavy foil or use regular foil folded to double thickness. Crisscross foil strips in spoke design and place pan on center of strips. Pull foil strips up and over pan.

Peach-Pecan Upside-Down Cake

Apple-Date Crisp

6 cups thinly sliced peeled apples (about
    6 medium apples, preferably Golden
    Delicious)
2 teaspoons lemon juice
⅓ cup chopped dates
1⅓ cups quick-cooking oats
½ cup all-purpose unbleached flour
½ cup packed light brown sugar
½ teaspoon ground cinnamon
¼ teaspoon ground ginger
¼ teaspoon salt
    Pinch ground nutmeg
    Pinch ground cloves (optional)
¼ cup (½ stick) cold butter, cut into small
    pieces

1. Spray slow cooker with nonstick cooking
spray. Place apples in medium bowl. Sprinkle
with lemon juice; toss to coat. Add dates and
mix well. Transfer apple mixture to slow cooker.

2. Combine oats, flour, brown sugar, cinnamon,
ginger, salt, nutmeg and cloves, if desired, in
medium bowl. Cut in butter with pastry blender
or two knives until mixture resembles coarse
crumbs.

3. Pour oat mixture into slow cooker over
apples; smooth top. Cover; cook on HIGH about
2 hours or on LOW about 4 hours or until apples
are tender. *Makes 6 servings*

Poached Pears with Raspberry Sauce

4 cups cran-raspberry juice cocktail
2 cups Rhine or Riesling wine
¼ cup sugar
2 cinnamon sticks, broken into halves
4 to 5 firm Bosc or Anjou pears, peeled
    and cored
1 package (10 ounces) frozen raspberries
    in syrup, thawed
    Fresh berries (optional)

1. Combine juice, wine, sugar and cinnamon
stick halves in slow cooker. Submerge pears in
mixture. Cover; cook on LOW 3½ to 4 hours or
until pears are tender. Remove and discard
cinnamon sticks.

2. Process raspberries in food processor or
blender until smooth; strain and discard seeds.
Spoon raspberry sauce onto serving plates;
place pear on top of sauce. Garnish with fresh
berries, if desired. *Makes 4 to 5 servings*

Apple-Date Crisp

Poached Pears with Raspberry Sauce

Baked Fudge Pudding Cake

    4 large eggs
1⅓ cups sugar
    1 cup unsalted butter, melted
    1 teaspoon vanilla
      Grated peel of 1 orange
    6 tablespoons unsweetened cocoa powder
    4 tablespoons all-purpose flour
      Dash of salt
  ½ cup heavy cream
      Chopped toasted pecans, whipped
        cream or vanilla ice cream (optional)

1. Spray inside of slow cooker with nonstick spray. Set slow cooker to LOW setting.

2. Beat eggs with electric mixer on medium-high speed until thickened. Gradually add sugar; beat for 5 minutes or until very thick and lemon-colored. Mix in butter, vanilla and peel.

3. Combine cocoa, flour and salt in small bowl. Stir cocoa mixture into egg mixture. Add heavy cream and mix until combined. Pour batter into slow cooker.

4. Before placing lid on slow cooker, cover opening with paper towel to collect condensation. Make sure paper towel does not touch pudding mixture. (Large slow cookers might require 2 connected paper towels.) Place lid on over paper towel. Cook on LOW 3 to 4 hours. (Do not cook on HIGH.) Sprinkle with pecans and serve with whipped cream or ice cream, if desired. Store leftover cake in a covered container in the refrigerator.

Makes 6 to 8 servings

Mixed Berry Cobbler

    1 package (16 ounces) frozen mixed
      berries
  ¾ cup granulated sugar
    2 tablespoons quick-cooking tapioca
    2 teaspoons grated fresh lemon peel
1½ cups all-purpose flour
  ½ cup packed brown sugar
2¼ teaspoons baking powder
  ¼ teaspoon ground nutmeg
  ¾ cup milk
  ⅓ cup butter or margarine, melted
      Ice cream (optional)

1. Stir together berries, granulated sugar, tapioca and lemon peel in slow cooker.

2. Combine flour, brown sugar, baking powder and nutmeg in medium bowl. Add milk and butter; stir just until blended. Drop spoonfuls on top of berry mixture.

3. Cover; cook on LOW 4 hours. Uncover; let stand about 30 minutes. Serve with ice cream, if desired.

Makes 8 servings

Mixed Berry Cobbler

Baked Ginger Apples

4 large Red Delicious apples
8 tablespoons (1 stick) unsalted butter, melted
⅓ cup chopped macadamia nuts
¼ cup chopped dried apricots
2 tablespoons finely chopped crystallized ginger
1 tablespoon dark brown sugar
¾ cup brandy
½ cup vanilla pudding and pie filling mix
2 cups heavy cream

1. Slice tops off apples and core. Combine butter, macadamia nuts, apricots, ginger and brown sugar in medium bowl. Fill apples with nut mixture.

2. Place apples in slow cooker. Pour brandy into slow cooker. Cover; cook on LOW 4 hours or on HIGH 2 hours.

3. Gently remove apples from slow cooker; set aside and keep warm. Combine pudding mix and cream in small bowl. Add to slow cooker; stir to combine with brandy. Cover; cook on HIGH 30 minutes. Stir until smooth.

4. Place apples in slow cooker and keep warm until ready to serve. Serve apples with cream mixture.   *Makes 4 servings*

Decadent Chocolate Delight

1 package chocolate cake mix
8 ounces sour cream
1 cup chocolate chips
1 cup water
4 eggs
¾ cup vegetable oil
1 package (4-serving size) chocolate flavor instant pudding and pie filling mix

1. Lightly grease inside of slow cooker.

2. Combine all ingredients in large bowl. Pour into slow cooker. Cover; cook on LOW 6 to 8 hours or on HIGH 3 to 4 hours. Serve hot or warm with ice cream.   *Makes 12 servings*

Baked Ginger Apple

Decadent Chocolate Delight

Chunky Sweet Spiced Apple Butter

4 cups (about 1¼ pounds) **peeled, chopped Granny Smith apples**
¾ cup packed dark brown sugar
2 tablespoons balsamic vinegar
¼ cup butter, divided
1 tablespoon ground cinnamon
½ teaspoon salt
¼ teaspoon ground cloves
1½ teaspoons vanilla

1. Combine apples, sugar, vinegar, 2 tablespoons butter, cinnamon, salt and cloves in slow cooker. Cover; cook on LOW 8 hours.

2. Stir in remaining 2 tablespoons butter and vanilla. Cool completely.   *Makes 2 cups*

Serving Suggestions: Serve with roasted meats or on toasted English muffins.

Easy Does It

Balsamic vinegar, the Italian condiment made from white Trebbiano grapes, gets its dark color and mellow flavor from aging in barrels. Unlike white vinegar, balsamic has a sweetness that works well with fruit.

English Bread Pudding

16 slices day-old, firm-textured white bread (1 small loaf)
1¾ cups milk
1 package (8 ounces) mixed dried fruit, cut into small pieces
½ cup chopped nuts
1 medium apple, cored and chopped
⅓ cup packed brown sugar
¼ cup butter, melted
1 egg, lightly beaten
1 teaspoon ground cinnamon
¼ teaspoon ground nutmeg
¼ teaspoon ground cloves

1. Tear bread, with crusts, into 1- to 2-inch pieces. Place in slow cooker. Pour milk over bread; let soak 30 minutes. Stir in dried fruit, nuts and apple.

2. Combine remaining ingredients in small bowl. Pour over bread mixture. Stir well to blend. Cover; cook on LOW 3½ to 4 hours or until skewer inserted in center comes out clean.
          Makes 6 to 8 servings

Note: Chopping dried fruits can be difficult. To make the job easier, cut the fruit with kitchen scissors. You can also spray your scissors or chef's knife with nonstick cooking spray before you begin chopping so that the fruit won't stick to the blade.

Chunky Sweet Spiced Apple Butter

Coconut Rice Pudding

    2 cups water
    1 cup uncooked long-grain rice
    1 tablespoon unsalted butter
      Pinch salt
   18 ounces evaporated milk
    1 can (14 ounces) cream of coconut
    ½ cup golden raisins
    3 egg yolks, beaten
      Grated peel of 2 limes
    1 teaspoon vanilla extract
      Toasted shredded coconut (optional)

1. Place water, rice, butter and salt in medium saucepan. Bring to a rolling boil over high heat, stirring frequently. Reduce heat to low. Cover; cook 10 to 12 minutes. Remove from heat. Let stand, covered, 5 minutes.

2. Meanwhile, spray slow cooker with nonstick cooking spray. Add evaporated milk, cream of coconut, raisins, egg yolks, lime peel and vanilla extract; mix well. Add rice; stir to combine. Cover; cook on LOW 4 hours or on HIGH 2 hours. Stir every 30 minutes, if possible. Pudding will thicken as it cools. Garnish with toasted shredded coconut, if desired.

Makes 6 (¾-cup) servings

Gingered Pineapple and Cranberries

    2 cans (20 ounces each) pineapple chunks
      in juice, undrained
    1 cup dried sweetened cranberries
    ½ cup brown sugar
    1 teaspoon curry powder, divided
    1 teaspoon grated fresh ginger, divided
    ¼ teaspoon red pepper flakes
    2 tablespoons water
    1 tablespoon cornstarch

1. Place pineapple with juice, cranberries, brown sugar, ½ teaspoon curry powder, ½ teaspoon ginger and pepper flakes into slow cooker. Cover; cook on HIGH 3 hours.

2. Combine water, cornstarch, remaining ½ teaspoon ginger and ½ teaspoon curry powder in small bowl; stir until cornstarch is dissolved. Add to pineapple mixture; cook on HIGH 15 minutes or until thickened

Makes 4½ cups

Variation: Substitute 2 cans (20 ounces each) pineapple tidbits in heavy syrup for pineapple and brown sugar.

Coconut Rice Pudding

Gingered Pineapple and Cranberries

Steamed Pumpkin Cake

1½ cups all-purpose flour
1½ teaspoons baking powder
1½ teaspoons baking soda
   1 teaspoon ground cinnamon
½ teaspoon salt
¼ teaspoon ground cloves
½ cup (1 stick) unsalted butter, melted
2 cups packed light brown sugar
3 eggs, beaten
1 can (15 ounces) pumpkin
   Sweetened whipped cream (optional)

1. Grease 2½-quart soufflé dish or baking pan that fits into slow cooker.

2. Combine flour, baking powder, baking soda, cinnamon, salt and cloves in medium bowl; set aside.

3. Beat butter, brown sugar and eggs in large bowl with electric mixer on medium speed until creamy. Beat in pumpkin. Stir in flour mixture. Spoon batter into prepared soufflé dish.

4. Add 1 inch hot water to slow cooker. Make foil handles to allow for easy removal of soufflé dish. Tear off three 18×2-inch strips of heavy foil or use regular foil folded to double thickness. Crisscross foil strips in spoke design and place soufflé dish on center of strips. Pull foil strips up and over dish. Place soufflé dish into slow cooker. Cover; cook on HIGH 3 to 3½ hours or until wooden toothpick inserted into center comes out clean.

5. Use foil handles to lift dish from slow cooker. Cool 15 minutes. Invert cake onto serving platter. Cut into wedges and serve with dollop of whipped cream, if desired.   *Makes 12 servings*

Serving Suggestion: Enhance this old-fashioned dense cake with a topping of sautéed apples or pear slices, or a scoop of pumpkin ice cream.

Peach Cobbler

2 packages (16 ounces each) frozen
   peaches, thawed and drained
¾ cup sugar
2 teaspoons ground cinnamon, divided
½ teaspoon ground nutmeg
¾ cup all-purpose flour
1 tablespoon sugar
6 tablespoons butter, cut into bits
   Whipped cream (if desired)

1. Combine peaches, sugar, 1½ teaspoons cinnamon and nutmeg in medium bowl. Place into slow cooker.

2. For topping, combine flour, sugar and remaining ½ teaspoon cinnamon in separate bowl. Cut in butter with pastry cutter or 2 knives until mixture resembles coarse crumbs. Sprinkle over peach mixture. Cover; cook on HIGH 2 hours. Serve with freshly whipped cream, if desired.   *Makes 4 to 6 servings*

Steamed Pumpkin Cake

Cran-Apple Orange Conserve

2 medium oranges
5 large tart apples, peeled, cored and chopped
2 cups sugar
1½ cups fresh cranberries
1 tablespoon grated fresh lemon peel
Pound cake

1. Remove a thin slice from both ends of both oranges for easier chopping. Finely chop unpeeled oranges and remove any seeds (You should have about 2 cups chopped orange.)

2. Combine oranges, apples, sugar, cranberries and lemon peel in slow cooker. Cover; cook on HIGH 4 hours. Slightly crush fruit with potato masher.

3. Cook, uncovered, on HIGH 2 to 2½ hours or until very thick, stirring occasionally to prevent sticking. Cool at least 2 hours. Serve with pound cake.   *Makes about 5 cups*

Spiced Plums and Pears

2 cans (29 ounces each) sliced pears in heavy syrup, undrained
2 pounds black or red plums (about 12 to 14), pitted and sliced
1 cup packed brown sugar
1 teaspoon ground cinnamon
½ teaspoon ground ginger
¼ teaspoon grated lemon peel
2 tablespoons cornstarch
2 tablespoons water
Pound cake or ice cream
Whipped topping

1. Cut pear slices in half with spoon. Place pears, plums, sugar, cinnamon, ginger and lemon peel in slow cooker. Cover; cook on HIGH 4 hours.

2. Combine cornstarch and water to make smooth paste. Stir into slow cooker. Cook on HIGH until slightly thickened.

3. Serve warm or at room temperature over pound cake with whipped topping.
Makes 6 to 8 servings

Easy Does It

Slow cookers turn out wonderful fruit conserves and relishes. Don't limit their use to dessert since many also work well as a sauce with grilled meat or fish.

Acknowledgments

The publisher would like to thank the companies and organizations listed below for the use of their recipes and photographs in this publication.

Campbell Soup Company

Perdue Farms Incorporated

Reckitt Benckiser Inc.

Metric Conversion Chart

VOLUME MEASUREMENTS (dry)

$1/8$ teaspoon = 0.5 mL
$1/4$ teaspoon = 1 mL
$1/2$ teaspoon = 2 mL
$3/4$ teaspoon = 4 mL
1 teaspoon = 5 mL
1 tablespoon = 15 mL
2 tablespoons = 30 mL
$1/4$ cup = 60 mL
$1/3$ cup = 75 mL
$1/2$ cup = 125 mL
$2/3$ cup = 150 mL
$3/4$ cup = 175 mL
1 cup = 250 mL
2 cups = 1 pint = 500 mL
3 cups = 750 mL
4 cups = 1 quart = 1 L

VOLUME MEASUREMENTS (fluid)

1 fluid ounce (2 tablespoons) = 30 mL
4 fluid ounces ($1/2$ cup) = 125 mL
8 fluid ounces (1 cup) = 250 mL
12 fluid ounces ($1 1/2$ cups) = 375 mL
16 fluid ounces (2 cups) = 500 mL

WEIGHTS (mass)

$1/2$ ounce = 15 g
1 ounce = 30 g
3 ounces = 90 g
4 ounces = 120 g
8 ounces = 225 g
10 ounces = 285 g
12 ounces = 360 g
16 ounces = 1 pound = 450 g

DIMENSIONS

$1/16$ inch = 2 mm
$1/8$ inch = 3 mm
$1/4$ inch = 6 mm
$1/2$ inch = 1.5 cm
$3/4$ inch = 2 cm
1 inch = 2.5 cm

OVEN TEMPERATURES

250°F = 120°C
275°F = 140°C
300°F = 150°C
325°F = 160°C
350°F = 180°C
375°F = 190°C
400°F = 200°C
425°F = 220°C
450°F = 230°C

BAKING PAN SIZES

Utensil	Size in Inches/Quarts	Metric Volume	Size in Centimeters
Baking or Cake Pan (square or rectangular)	8×8×2	2 L	20×20×5
	9×9×2	2.5 L	23×23×5
	12×8×2	3 L	30×20×5
	13×9×2	3.5 L	33×23×5
Loaf Pan	8×4×3	1.5 L	20×10×7
	9×5×3	2 L	23×13×7
Round Layer Cake Pan	8×1½	1.2 L	20×4
	9×1½	1.5 L	23×4
Pie Plate	8×1¼	750 mL	20×3
	9×1¼	1 L	23×3
Baking Dish or Casserole	1 quart	1 L	—
	1½ quart	1.5 L	—
	2 quart	2 L	—